The Privatisation of Indigenous Land Tenure and the Future of African Indigenous Law

Enyinna Nwauche

The Privatisation of Indigenous Land Tenure and the Future of African Indigenous Law

Springer

Enyinna Nwauche
Faculty of Law
University of Fort Hare
East London, South Africa

ISBN 978-3-032-14880-3 ISBN 978-3-032-14881-0 (eBook)
https://doi.org/10.1007/978-3-032-14881-0

This Springer imprint is published by the registered company Springer Nature Switzerland AG
The registered company address is: Gewerbestrasse 11, 6330 Cham, Switzerland

Dedicated
to
Gordon Woodman
and
Thomas Bennett

Preface

This book examines the future of indigenous law in Africa through the lens of the privatisation of indigenous land tenure, which is arguably the most significant fact of the post-colonial indigenous law in Africa. It is therefore fitting, almost three decades after the beginning of the systematic and widespread statutory development of indigenous land tenure, to determine whether privatisation of indigenous land tenure destroyed, altered, amended, or improved indigenous law through a legislative process that has been a matter of relief, controversy, concern, exasperation, and frustration. The central question this book addresses is: What remains of indigenous law in the wake of the privatisation of indigenous land tenure? This question has largely escaped serious scrutiny because the enormous literature on indigenous tenure reform in Africa has proceeded without serious concern for the indigenous law framework that underpins indigenous law reform. Several reform proposals have been reactions to the principles of indigenous law, yet the fate of this law is ignored and treated with contempt in several African states. There are other African states where the survival of the indigenous community has framed the development of indigenous law and the privatisation of land tenure. The diversity of approaches in the statutory reform of indigenous land tenure strongly suggests the need for critical reflections on models of privatisation; the management of indigenous tenure; whether marginalised stakeholders, such as women, have access to indigenous land tenure; the process of settling tenure disputes, and the recording and registration of indigenous land tenure.

The tentative conclusion that this book interrogates is that indigenous law has modestly thrived in several African states, such as Uganda, Ghana, Kenya, and Tanzania, where the survival of communities and their laws has been seriously factored into the privatisation process. There are considerable problems in several other African states, such as Nigeria, that have privatised indigenous land tenure with little regard for the survival of indigenous communities and their laws.

Ideas about how to balance concern for individual growth with communal survival are the focus of several parts of this book. Even in states that have indigenous communities in mind, there is slow progress towards a sustainable framework of indigenous land tenure that recognises privatisation. In several parts of Africa, there are community members who can utilise indigenous land tenure to their benefit with the consent of their community. Even ideas and processes about how this could be implemented are undeveloped or impeded by bureaucratic constraints, notably the lack of adequate resources required to document indigenous land tenure, for example. This point is made to emphasise the gap in achieving a balance between individual interest and communal integrity in the privatisation process.

This book is a modest contribution to the enormous literature on land tenure in Africa. It draws attention to Africa's plural legal regimes and the need to constantly interrogate the future of the different legal orders in general and of indigenous law, which is paradoxically the majority legal order but inferior to state law and practice, even in African states that have constitutionalised indigenous law. This book advocates for the reimagination of a multi-stakeholder-managed tenure process as part of a broader pursuit for a moral order within indigenous communities guided by the norms of solidarity, care, compassion, and sustenance as reflected in the relationships fostered through property relations.

In this book, the term 'indigenous' is used in preference to 'native', 'customary', 'traditional', and 'endogenous' to describe the normative framework of indigenous communities in Africa. There are references to 'customary' law, especially in numerous legislations.

Chapter "The Privatisation of Indigenous Land Tenure Development and the Future of African Indigenous Law" of this book provides a wide context for how the future of indigenous laws in Africa is tied to the privatisation of indigenous land tenure, by exploring the development of indigenous law, indigenous property, and other features of indigenous law that have a direct bearing on privatisation. Chapter "An Overview of Indigenous Land Tenure in Africa" concentrates on the features of indigenous land tenure and how they contribute to privatisation and the future of indigenous land tenure. In addition, it is demonstrated that individual and communal tenure remain as old as Africa and that privatisation of land tenure is not a novel phenomenon in land tenure in Africa. The models of private interests in indigenous land tenure in Africa are the focus of chapter "Models of Private Interests in Indigenous Land Tenure in Africa", which partly engages with the form and substance of the privatisation of indigenous land tenure in Africa. Two models are identified and explored through a review of secondary literature. The model of private interests in communally owned indigenous land tenure is demonstrated by examining the legislative developments in Ghana, Kenya, Uganda, and South Africa. The second model demonstrates the impact of state ownership of land tenure and the privatisation of indigenous tenure in Mozambique, Angola, Nigeria, Tanzania, Botswana, Namibia, and Ethiopia.

No meaningful discussion of the future of African indigenous law can occur without a discussion of patriarchy and gender equality generally and how access to indigenous land tenure has unfolded as African states recognise women's individual titles and rights as citizens. Chapter "Patriarchy, Gender, and Access to Indigenous Land Tenure in Africa" of the book engages with this discussion through a thematic discussion of women's access to indigenous land tenure in several African states. These issues include the constitutional recognition of equality in spousal property, inheritance rights, and women's membership of indigenous land management bodies. Chapter "Compulsory Acquisition of Indigenous Land Tenure in African States" considers how the compulsory acquisition of indigenous land tenure impacts the privatisation of land tenure. The recording of indigenous land tenure is the focus of chapter "Documentation and Registration of Indigenous Land Tenure", which addresses the difficulty of determining individual title where there is insufficient evidence of the communal land tenure. Chapter "Arbitration and Adjudication of Indigenous Land Tenure Disputes" of the book addresses the arbitration and adjudication of indigenous land tenure disputes as a means of norm-making and a significant internal process that helps define the future of indigenous law in plural African states. Chapter "The Privatisation of Land Tenure and the Future of Indigenous Law in Africa" returns to the future of indigenous law by reimagining indigenous communities as moral communities in Africa.

It is important to caution the reader that this book has several limitations, including a scarcity of examples, due in part to language differences and the vast diversity across 53 African countries and over 3000 indigenous communities. The reader is encouraged to consult the extensive body of literature on land tenure in Africa.

East London, South Africa Enyinna S. Nwauche
December 2025

Acknowledgement

This book was conceived during a sabbatical leave in 2023. I spent part of that leave at the Faculty of Law, University of Toronto. I owe a debt of gratitude to Associate Dean Christopher Essert, Professor Anna Su, and Cathy Alzner for hosting me as a visiting professor of law. My original intent was to compare the privatisation of indigenous land tenure in Commonwealth Africa and Canada. It became clear early in the preparation of the work that a first step towards such a comparative work is to reflect first on what the privatisation of indigenous land tenure means for Africa.

I am grateful to Professors Asonzeh Ukah, Achike Agbakoba, and Anthony Diala, who, in one way or another, facilitated the completion of the book.

The late Gordon Woodman and Thomas Bennett, to whom this book is dedicated, are visionaries who saw a future for African indigenous law and devoted their academic careers to that enterprise.

I thank Springer for editorial guidance. Laura Hofmann has been kind and patient in guiding me through the process at Springer, and I am grateful. I am also grateful to Tanja Botha and the anonymous reviewers who understood the book's intent.

I remain responsible for all the errors in the book.

Contents

The Privatisation of Indigenous Land Tenure Development and the Future of African Indigenous Law 1
1 Introduction 1
2 Indigenous Law in Constant Flux: The Development of Indigenous Law in Africa 2
3 Is Indigenous Property Conceived as Constitutional Property in Recognition of Its Foundational Resource of Indigenous Law? 8
4 An Enhanced and Reimagined Vision of Indigenous Communities 10
5 The Catalytic Effect of the Regional and International Protection of Indigenous Property 14
6 Conclusion 16
References 17

An Overview of Indigenous Land Tenure in Africa 19
1 Introduction 19
2 Communal Ownership and Management of Indigenous Land Tenure 20
3 Access and Secondary Rights in Indigenous Land Tenure 23
4 Marginalised Stakeholders and Access to Indigenous Land Tenure 24
5 The Oral and Undocumented Nature of Indigenous Land Tenure 25
6 The Sacred Nature of Indigenous Land Tenure 26
7 A Longitudinal Overview of the Privatisation of Indigenous Land Tenure in Africa 26
8 Conclusion 30
References 31

Models of Private Interests in Indigenous Land Tenure in Africa 33
1 Introduction 33
2 Private Interests in Communally Indigenous Land Tenure 34
2.1 Ghana 34
2.2 Kenya 39
2.3 Uganda 45
2.4 South Africa 49
2.5 Liberia 54
2.6 Sierra Leone 56
2.7 Tanzania 57
3 State Ownership and Privatised Indigenous Land Tenure 59
3.1 Mozambique 59
3.2 Angola 60
3.3 Nigeria 61
3.4 Botswana 64
3.5 Namibia 67
3.6 Ethiopia 68
3.7 Zimbabwe 73
4 An Assessment of the Future of Indigenous Law in Africa through the Models of Privatisation of Indigenous Land Tenure in Africa 77
5 Conclusion 81
References 82

Patriarchy, Gender, and Access to Indigenous Land Tenure in Africa ... 87
1 Introduction 87
2 Constitutional Frameworks for Gender Equality 90
3 Statutory Recognition of Women's Access to Indigenous Land Tenure 92
4 Conclusion 96
References 97

Compulsory Acquisition of Indigenous Land Tenure in African States .. 99
1 Introduction 99
2 Indigenous Land Tenure and Elements of Compulsory Acquisition of Indigenous Lands in Africa 100
2.1 Legality 101
2.2 Determining 'Public Purpose' for Expropriating Indigenous Land 101
2.3 Procedure for Compulsory Acquisition 103
2.4 Payment of Compensation 107
2.5 Subsequent Use of Compulsorily Acquired Indigenous Land 110

3 Have African Judiciaries and Governments Failed Indigenous Peoples in the Large-Scale Acquisition of Indigenous Lands? 110
4 Conclusion 111
References... 111

Documentation and Registration of Indigenous Land Tenure 113
1 Introduction... 113
2 State Practice in the Documentation and Registration of Indigenous Land Tenure 115
3 Issues from State Practice................................ 121
3.1 Significant Orally Held Communal Indigenous Land Tenure in Africa 122
3.2 Establishing an Indigenous Land Records Registry.......... 122
3.3 Abdication of Indigenous Communities of their Obligation to Record their Indigenous Land Tenure 123
3.4 Consulting Traditional Authorities in Documenting and Registering Indigenous Land Tenure 123
4 Conclusion 123
References... 124

Arbitration and Adjudication of Indigenous Land Tenure Disputes 127
1 Introduction... 127
2 Family and Communal Arbitration over Indigenous Land Tenure in African States 128
3 Local Land Management Institutions and Dispute Settlement of Indigenous Land Tenure Disputes............................ 131
4 The Unlimited Jurisdiction of State Courts Over Indigenous Land Tenure Disputes 133
5 Conclusion 138
References... 138

The Privatisation of Land Tenure and the Future of Indigenous Law in Africa 141
1 The Privatisation of Land Tenure and the Future of Indigenous Law in Africa 141

The Privatisation of Indigenous Land Tenure Development and the Future of African Indigenous Law

Contents

1 Introduction 1
2 Indigenous Law in Constant Flux: The Development of Indigenous Law in Africa 2
3 Is Indigenous Property Conceived as Constitutional Property in Recognition of Its Foundational Resource of Indigenous Law? 8
4 An Enhanced and Reimagined Vision of Indigenous Communities 10
5 The Catalytic Effect of the Regional and International Protection of Indigenous Property. 14
6 Conclusion 16
References 17

1 Introduction

In this book, it is argued that the widespread privatisation of indigenous land tenure is an important and necessary process and has generally led to the development of African indigenous law; a promising indicator for its future. In examining the future of African indigenous law, the author acknowledges the fact that the legislative privatisation of indigenous land tenure in Africa is arguably the most significant fact of Africa's post-colonial indigenous law. It is therefore fitting, almost three decades after the organised commencement of the statutory reform of indigenous land tenure, to determine whether the privatisation of indigenous land tenure destroyed, altered, amended, or improved indigenous law through a legislative process that has been a matter of relief, controversy, concern, exasperation, and frustration. The central question to address is this: What remains of indigenous law in the wake of the privatisation of indigenous land tenure? Other related questions include the following: What is needed for the successful privatisation of indigenous land tenure so that the latter survives and thrives in African states? Are there lessons of the privatisation process, whether determined as a failed model or a success for future legislative reform? In this chapter, context is provided for a reasoned answer to these questions by examining the nature and features of indigenous law in Africa. In the next part,

E. Nwauche, *The Privatisation of Indigenous Land Tenure and the Future of African Indigenous Law*, https://doi.org/10.1007/978-3-032-14881-0_1

the development of indigenous law in Africa is considered. The idea of a constitutional indigenous property is then considered. The importance of an enhanced and reimagined indigenous community is next considered. Finally, the catalytic effect of the regional and international protection of indigenous property is discussed.

2 Indigenous Law in Constant Flux: The Development of Indigenous Law in Africa

As stated above, widespread legislative change in indigenous law is a tool that African legislatures resorted to, to reflect enormous changes in the political, social, economic, and cultural life of Africans.[1] States rather than indigenous communities are champions of these changes because of the widespread belief that the organic development of indigenous law is often frustratingly slow and cannot keep pace with developments. Such a view also imagines African societies as monolithic and that African indigenous laws reflect unanimous normative understanding. However, African societies, like all societies, are in constant change, such that norms are constructed, contested, challenged, and disobeyed, so that what we may regard as living customary law—increasingly accepted as the preferred form of customary law—also reflects patriarchal inequalities, bias, oppression, and discrimination of women and other vulnerable groups in many indigenous communities. For example, even though the idea that African indigenous communities are patriarchal is true, it is greatly contested in many African communities and in no way truly represents the views of a majority of African indigenous communities that claim and observe the values of equality, dignity, and solidarity as fundamental organising principles.

Primarily, legislative reform of indigenous law in Africa often captures social changes in indigenous societies. It is, of course, true that there is considerable opposition to such changes, ranging from accusations of contemptible interference by state law, unacceptable modelling of indigenous law on Western frameworks, the neo-liberal hegemony of the Global North as a form of cultural warfare, and that considerable changes to indigenous law suggest that they have become state law.[2] There are very good things to learn from this criticism. However, the fundamental point is that these reforms are made by democratically elected representatives, and available evidence suggests a modest positive impact in several areas of the privatisation of indigenous peoples, such as land tenure, family, and property law. A brief overview of the legislative reforms of indigenous law is important, at least to demonstrate the constant flux of indigenous law and show that the privatisation of indigenous land tenure is a feature of such development.

[1] See the following: Kerr (2009), pp. 677–689; Knoetze and Olivier (2005) Obiter 126–132.

[2] These ideas are explored in more detail in chapter "An Overview of Indigenous Land Tenure in Africa" of this book.

Concerning the reform of family law, legislative reforms in Kenya, Zimbabwe, Senegal, Tanzania, Mozambique, Côte d'Ivoire, Eswatini, South Africa, Nigeria, Ghana, Malawi, Botswana, Niger Republic, and Mali have enacted reforms with respect to marriage, inheritance, the minimum age of marriage, marital power and property, discriminatory practices, and succession.[3] These legislations complement constitutional guarantees and judicial protection of gender equality, dignity, and freedom from discrimination, such that, across Africa, women have successfully engaged patriarchy and other forms of discrimination, which demonstrates that patriarchy is not a fundamental construct of African indigenous laws that can thrive without male dominance. To be clear, there is considerable resistance to these reforms from indigenous communities and other stakeholders. Legislation has often been used to address rules to validate the application of indigenous law, prohibit harmful cultural practices,[4] and reform customary property succession regimes.[5] Therefore, it was not surprising that the privatisation of indigenous land tenure has occurred through statutory reform. It is often assumed that states undertaking statutory reform possess the necessary skills to ensure that the outcomes of such processes express both the will of the state and the normative frameworks of indigenous communities. Another assumption would be a clearly defined and operational indigenous law sector that would respond to statutory interventions. A third assumption is the purposeful judicial interpretation of statutory rules, bearing in mind the legislative intent and stakeholder interests. Since legislation is often episodic, judicial interpretation remains a fundamental part of the reform process.

Colonialism as a process was an unwelcome development of customary law, in general, and, in particular, featured mandates to develop indigenous law, which is also a feature of post-colonial African states. Although colonial Africa required African judiciaries to apply recognition tests such as the notorious repugnancy clause that generally permitted African judiciaries to apply native law and custom that was equitable in good conscience and in accordance with the dictates of natural justice, post-colonial African states retained these clauses in several states[6] and also used the Bill of Rights as a standard to evaluate and develop principles of African

[3] See for example, Fenrich et al. (2013); Diala (2021).

[4] Examples include the management of initiation rites in South Africa (see South Africa's Customary Initiation Act 2021); the abolition of female genital mutilation in African States (see Kenya's Prohibition of Female Genital Mutilation Act 2022; The Prohibition of Female Genital Mutilation Act 2010; Tanzania's Sexual Offences Special Provisions Act 1998; Ghana's Criminal and Other Offences Act 1960, and Domestic Violence Act 2007; Nigeria's The Violence Against Persons (Prohibition) Act 2015; and South Africa's The Promotion of Equality and Prevention of Unfair Discrimination Act 4 of 2000); the management of child bride marriages (see Ghana's Criminal Code (Amendment) Act 1998 abolishing the Trokosi brides).

[5] See for example, the Reform of Customary Law of Succession and Regulation of Related Matters Act of 2009 promulgated by the South African parliament, mandated by South Africa's Constitutional Court in the case of *Bhe v Magistrate, Khayelitsha* (2005) 1 SA 580 (CC).

[6] See for example Kenya's Judicature Act in sect 3(2) provides that: 'The High Court, the Court of Appeal and all subordinate courts shall be guided by African customary law in civil cases in which one or more of the parties is subject to it or affected by it, so far as it is applicable and is not repug-

indigenous laws.[7] In some states, such as South Africa,[8] there is a clear constitutional duty to develop African indigenous law. Even in other African states with an indirect mandate to develop customary law, the nature of these mandates is unclear as to how to interpret provisions of the statutory reform of indigenous law within a human rights paradigm. Rather than imagining human rights as opposed to indigenous law, usually expressed in the cliche that human rights are individualistic and indigenous law is communal, the principles, values, and processes of indigenous law can be of great assistance in articulating the content of different human rights. This enormously difficult task is underway in many states, but at a disagreeable pace.

All indigenous law is socially constructed, none more so than African indigenous laws. African indigenous law theorists, such as Martin Chanock,[9] Gordon Woodman,[10] Thomas Bennett, Anthony Allot,[11] and Teslim O Elias,[12] have demonstrated in different ways and forms that African indigenous law principles, values, and institutions are creations of Africans led and, in some cases, assisted by co-creators such as colonial states, post-colonial African states, and the international community.[13]

This section sketches a broad overview of the factors that affect the development of indigenous law in general. The first point is that the subject of reform is of considerable importance but occurs as stated above in a social context. Although indigenous land tenure is part of customary property, the former has become synonymous with communal property. Customary property in Africa represents things of value, material and immaterial, to Africa's indigenous communities, ranging from land, animals, chattels, knowledge systems, and money.[14] The considerable importance of indigenous property is its foundation in indigenous law and communities in Africa. Indigenous property serves as a bond of solidarity and sustenance enabling several indigenous communities to thrive because of its communal ethos. However, this same ethos can frustrate those members who are unable or ill-equipped to access such communal resources for their own sustenance. This tension has always attended collective properties and has been a constant feature of indigenous property in Africa. This book determines what may be a fair balance between the tension and individual interests within a communal land tenure system. Should a communal property system be abolished to allow individual interests to thrive, or should an

nant to justice and morality or inconsistent with any written law, and shall decide all such cases according to substantial justice without undue regard to technicalities of procedure and undue delay.'

[7] See generally the following works by Bennett (1995, 2004, 2009).

[8] See sect 39(2) of the South African Constitution, which requires the South African judiciary, when developing customary law, to promote the spirit, purport, and objects of the Bill of Rights.

[9] See the following works of Chanock (1985, 2001).

[10] See the following works by Woodman (1969, 2001). Woodman (1985), pp. 143–163. Woodman (1988), pp. 181–220. Woodman (1995), pp. 5–24. Woodman (1996).

[11] Allot (1985), Allot (1965a), p. 216; Allot (1965b), p. 366; Allot (1977).

[12] See the following work by Elias (1956).

[13] See also Snyder (1981).

[14] See generally, Chanock (1991).

individual tenure be allowed to thrive within the communal property system? The ensuing chapters of this book show different approaches to this question, varying from state to state and from period to period. Part of what this book addresses is the nature and extent to which indigenous land tenure has thrived, survived, or disappeared as privatisation, defined simply as the recognition of private interests from hitherto communal land tenure. If indigenous law has survived or disappeared, how did that happen? Was it through an express legislative intent, judicial development, or an organic development by indigenous communities of origin? If African judiciaries have contributed to the defence or disappearance of such tenure, what tools and strategies have they deployed? Are these tools constitutionally or statutorily based, or are they innovative? Are principles such as patriarchy immutable or socially constructed, as several African states legislate the privatisation of communal indigenous land tenure across Africa?

Indigenous law is arguably the majority legal order in Africa by reason of population, but paradoxically, the inferior legal order in all African states in practice. The privatisation of the communal land tenure demonstrates the promise and peril of indigenous laws in Africa's plural legal orders. As an inferior legal order, there is always the possibility that indigenous law becomes appropriated by the dominant legal order in African states. It is not surprising that claims of appropriation and homogenisation of Africa's plural legal systems in the image of received civil and common law are rampant. If plural African legal states prefer to use legislation as a technique to develop indigenous law, in general, it is expected that the dominant legal order would be the frame of reference. The oral nature of indigenous law highlights the inferior status of indigenous law in Africa. African courts struggle to ascertain indigenous law. In the context of our discussions about the privatisation of indigenous land tenure, it is evident that indigenous property jurisprudence has facilitated the growth of indigenous land tenure in several African countries. There is little doubt that the codification of the principles of indigenous land tenure will be of assistance as interpretative guides for African courts as they engage with indigenous land tenure legislations. While it is true that the flexibility and nuances of African customary law may be lost through such intervention, it is also true that, since African legal orders operate in a written environment, the survival of indigenous law lies within some form of codification or writing.

In determining the principles of indigenous African law, in some states, a distinction has arisen between the 'official' and 'living' law. The argument is that the fluid, flexible, and negotiable way that indigenous law is constructed and co-constructed by communities represents the living law. Official customary law is a broad term of state-sanctioned codes of indigenous law that misrepresent the true nature of indigenous law. It appears that the principles of indigenous law lie somewhere in between. On the one hand, the oral nature of indigenous law is one of its significant drawbacks in a legal system where writing and formalisation are the norm. What is oral is challenging to comprehend, study, preserve, and protect. If indigenous law is to apply in African courts, the sources of such law, including state-sanctioned codes and writings, are welcome as part of the evidentiary process. The sources and social dynamics of state-sanctioned codes must be interrogated before their application.

Questions about the provenance of the codes are important and provide a basis for critical inquiry. This foundation facilitates the massive task of capturing the nuances, perspectives, deflections, and negotiations that characterise indigenous law. On the other hand, one of the dangers of the 'living' law is the possibility that what is presented as 'living' law may represent sectional views and interpretations of what is fluid, flexible, and negotiable. The belief that people who live customary law know it does not translate into a proper representation of that 'lived' law in the world. Living customary law points to realities that are often distorted and reflect all the symmetries in African indigenous communities with discrimination, a lack of transparency, and patriarchy.

The oral nature of African indigenous law reflects a broader challenge—the lack of written records that characterises indigenous communities asserting knowledge of the title and plans of customary properties. While tangible customary properties, such as houses, are easy to determine, communal and family land may be difficult to settle with the certainty that third parties may demand. The impact of inadequate documentation of customary property presents enormous challenges to the property regimes of African legal systems that thrive on certainty and boundaries. The many difficulties of documenting indigenous land tenure include the capacity of existing documentation mechanisms to reflect indigenous land tenure, the appropriate party to represent different types of indigenous tenure, and the means to capture multiple and interlocking interests that may exist in family and communal land. "In several African states that constitutionally recognise indigenous law as a source of law in the legal system equal to other sources of law, including the civil and common law—such as South Africa and Kenya—indigenous law is required to pass certain validity and evidentiary tests to be applicable in African courts."[15] Indigenous law is at the mercy of African courts whose interpretative duties have an impact on how indigenous law is operationalised within plural legal systems. The extent to which African judiciaries have engaged in the statutory interpretation of legislation privatising communal land tenure is slowly unravelling, even if it is clear that these courts are potentially important in ensuring that indigenous law survives privatisation.

In many African states, multiple indigenous laws are the foundation of indigenous property. Indigenous law springs from the collective understanding of an ethnic community. An ethnic community is a people bound together by a culture that reflects a shared understanding manifested in cultural, linguistic, and physiological facts. Although this is an incomplete definition, it is a guide towards understanding the enormous diversity of ethnic groups in Africa that number thousands. Does the multiplicity affect a coherent articulation of indigenous laws, and perhaps a key question is whether it is important to achieve this articulation? In a sense, developing indigenous African laws could be a daunting challenge. However, it appears that the differences in African indigenous law may seem exaggerated, and a process of homogenisation of indigenous laws has occurred in African states as a result of the

[15] See for example Art. 2(4) and Art 11(1) of the 2010 Kenyan Constitution as well as Sec. 211(3) of the 1996 Constitution of the Republic of South Africa.

statutory development and implementation of different aspects of indigenous law. Examples range from the principles of dispute settlement, the conditions for the sale of indigenous land, indigenous tenancy, and the rule of primogeniture in intestate succession. The multiplicity of indigenous laws presents a challenge to whether development must be preceded by the determination of indigenous laws. The risks and challenges for the statutory development of indigenous laws in Africa are evident.

Another feature of African indigenous laws is their flexibility. There appear to be two senses in which indigenous law is said to be flexible. In one sense, it is put forward that the flexibility of customary law is one of its enduring advantages. Flexibility underscores the ability to resolve disputes in a wholesome manner with the aim of reconciling the parties in a socially acceptable way. There are no victor and no vanquished parties, but a harmonious family or community. This meant a reliance on substance rather than on strict procedure. But this was only natural. Until colonial enterprise began to take effect, traditional institutions such as the traditional ruler in council dispensed customary law; the family, the elders' council, the men and women's meeting, which operated in an informal manner that took special cognisance of the peculiar facts of a case and did not rely on the rules of precedent. Furthermore, the oral nature of customary law ensured that there was ample discretion in the hands of dispute settlement bodies able to make decisions that were considered to be fair. Whether this sense of the flexibility of indigenous law should guide and affect the development of indigenous laws is a continuing problem and must be borne in mind as development and implementation occur. Another sense of the flexibility of customary law is often pejorative, hinting at the uncertainty of indigenous law and the fact that it has little structure to be studied and analysed. If a law changed from time to time, it would lose the certainty that is crucial in the way individuals and communities order their existence.

Indigenous law in Africa is important because of its normative foundations in more than 3,000 ethnic groups in Africa in 53 states that speak more than 2100 languages constituting more than 90% of an estimated population of Africa's 1.2 billion people, with roughly half of this population living in urban areas occupying a land mass of 30.37 million square kilometres. It is also estimated that over half of land tenure in Africa is indigenous land tenure in a continent that, on all indices, is underdeveloped and beset with significant political, socio-economic, and governance crises. Therefore, it is not surprising that changing the character and nature of indigenous land tenure, which is foundation in these communities, was identified as a harbinger of social and economic change if ordinary Africans could be empowered to create wealth through the use of their land tenure.[16] One option open to African states was to allow the organic and incremental development of indigenous law or to turn to the privatisation of indigenous land tenure.

[16] See for example, McAuslan (2015), pp. 339–357; Wily (2012); Knight (2010); Chimhowu (2019), p. 897; Wily (2011), p. 733. Cotula (2007).

3 Is Indigenous Property Conceived as Constitutional Property in Recognition of Its Foundational Resource of Indigenous Law?

This section addresses the constitutionalisation of indigenous law in general and indigenous property in particular.[17] At the heart of the constitutionalisation of indigenous property is the clash between the liberal ethos of African constitutions and the communal character of indigenous property.

The constitutional protection of indigenous property is important for many reasons. First, it is assumed that a constitution regards indigenous property as equal to other private property regimes. The implications of this statement are evident in a number of ways, including an obligation on the state to ensure that some of the features of private property are extended to indigenous land tenure. Mechanisms such as registration and titling are in focus here. Second, constitutional visions of indigenous property vary between a constitutional vision of ownership and management of indigenous lands by indigenous communities and a vision of state ownership of indigenous property. Third, the manner in which indigenous property is recognised is crucial in evaluating whether legislation in furtherance of indigenous property meets the constitutional standards. Fourth, the constitutional requirement of non-discrimination becomes implied in the management of indigenous property. Consequently, much of the access that African judiciaries have granted to women, girls, and other marginalised persons has been based on the rights to dignity, equality, and non-discrimination. It is, of course, important to state that without constitutionalisation, these rights will be available to all citizens, but constitutionalising indigenous property elevates the status of indigenous property. Fifth, it appears to be an additional advantage if a constitution mandates legislation to elaborate on the protection of indigenous tenure, as in the case of Kenya, where Article 63(5) of the 2010 Constitution mandates legislation to provide for community land[18] which vests in and is held by communities identified based on ethnicity, culture, or similar community of interest. This legislation should provide that community land shall not be disposed of or used in any way except in the manner that the legislation sets out the nature and extent of the rights of members individually and collectively. In essence, this is an excellent example of a constitutional vision of privatised indigenous land tenure. The Kenyan 2016 Community Land Act was made in furtherance of this provision and is considered in chapter "Models of Private Interests in Indigenous Land Tenure in Africa" of this book.

Communal ownership of indigenous property is a fundamental principle of indigenous African law because of the social, economic, and political tasks that communal property performs in African societies. Indigenous land provides economic sustenance for indigenous societies that are primarily agrarian. It provided

[17] See generally Mqeke (2009), p. 689; Rautenbach (1999), pp. 113–132.

[18] See the Community Land Act 2016.

materials for shelter and defined the social kinship of family and community members. Succession and inheritance revolved around land tenure. Patriarchy and male primogeniture as principles of succession and inheritance arose because male prowess is imagined to be better suited to exploiting and protecting land tenure. The community and family members have access rights determined by norms continuously developed and negotiated by family and community members. Land tenure is crucial to the harmony of communities and in its communal character it is even more so. Whether post-colonial African constitutions recognise the fundamental nature of indigenous property is debatable and provides a serious fault line in the development and protection of indigenous land tenure. Some appropriate questions include whether the constitutional protection of property appropriately reflects the communal ethos of indigenous property. The difficulty in reconciling an individually orientated property clause with a communally orientated property regime is easy to imagine. The question that may be asked is whether privatisation is in furtherance of indigenous property as a constitutional right? If the right to property is a constitutional right, it stands to reason that constitutional property should be examined like all other rights or as a unique set of rights. It is therefore important to determine whether constitutional property is conceived as private individual property or collectivist in nature. If it is collectivist in nature, indigenous property could be a special type of constitutional property that privileges collectivism to the detriment of individual interests. Such a collective vision of indigenous property would not be strange since several collectivist types of property recognise property held by and/or for the benefit of groups of people. As the next paragraph reveals, there is hardly any mention of indigenous property in African constitutions. What appears are visions of land tenure in different constitutions and suggest that visions of land tenure could be a substitute for visions of property. For example, Section 60 of the Constitution of the Republic of Kenya 2010 captures the objectives of indigenous land tenure reform that could easily pass for a constitutional vision of property in Africa. That vision includes a requirement that land is to be held, used, and managed in an equitable, efficient, productive, and sustainable manner, following equitable access to land; security of land rights; sustainable and productive management of land resources; transparent and cost-effective administration of land; sound conservation and protection of ecologically sensitive areas; elimination of gender discrimination in law, customs, and practices related to land and property in land; and settlement of land disputes through constitutionally compliant local community initiatives. The absence of clear visions of property in African constitutions is, therefore, regrettable, as is the conflation of property and land tenure in these constitutions.

Several countries recognise indigenous land tenure directly as part of the protection of property or through stand-alone clauses. Several other countries recognise indigenous land tenure through the recognition of culture as a value or through the judicial enforcement of indigenous law and references to property legislation. Relevant questions include whether direct or indirect recognition of indigenous land tenure amounts to a particular understanding of constitutional property different from what has become an orthodox understanding of constitutional property that situates indigenous land tenure as the tension and balance between individual and communal understandings of property. Further questions include whether the legislative development of indigenous land tenure is an inevitable path of constitutional indigenous property. What can be further asked are the constitutional standards to guide the legislative development of indigenous land tenure.

Examples of the constitutional property clause in African states include the Ugandan Constitution, which recognises a customary land tenure system.[19] South Sudan, which recognises community land[20] defined as including all lands traditionally and historically held or used by local communities and their members. In Ghana, Article 36(8) recognises stool skin[21] and family lands as indigenous tenure.[22] Angola constitutionally recognises land held by rural communities.[23] In Ethiopia, private property includes 'lands held … in appropriate circumstances … by communities specifically empowered by law to own property in common'.[24] The Zambian Constitution also recognises customary land.[25] These examples further illustrate the conflation of property and land as stated above. A constitutional vision of property would include other forms of property.

4 An Enhanced and Reimagined Vision of Indigenous Communities

An enhanced standing for communities that occupy an amorphous space between the individual and the state in Africa is important in an optimal framework for the privatisation of indigenous land tenure. Such an optimal framework would promote the privatisation of indigenous land tenure ensuring the survival of the community. The importance of property in constituting liberal democratic economies is not in dispute and is as important to communities as it is to individuals. The reality that communities are fit and separate subjects of legal systems is not adequately acknowledged. If it were, and as stated above, privatisation would occur without destroying communities.

A reimagined indigenous community could establish an appropriate political structure of indigenous communities that promotes self-governance and limited autonomy within a state through enhanced management of indigenous land tenure. Realising the potential of self-governance of indigenous communities in Africa requires an articulation of measures designed to ensure that broad-based

[19] See art 237(4) of the 1995 Uganda Constitution.

[20] Article 171(2) of the South Sudan Constitution.

[21] Stool and skin lands are traditional forms of land ownership.

[22] See art 36(8) of the 1992 Ghana Constitution.

[23] See art 98(1) of the Angolan Constitution.

[24] See art 40(2) of the Ethiopian Constitution.

[25] See art 254(1) of the Zambian Constitution.

governance structures involving women and youth are implemented to ensure that indigenous land tenure fosters and sustains the community, where private interests not only express the individual's right but also the burden of responsibilities/duties. The questions of gender access and asymmetrical power relations[26] in communities are part of the issues around the ownership and management of communal land tenure, where the individual title is recognised. For example, there is evidence in Southern Africa of abuse of land governance by traditional authorities[27] and it may be asked whether land tenure management should be insulated from traditional authorities to ensure greater representation of stakeholders. Yet, other questions include the plausibility of contemplating non-members of the community as stakeholders. Different perspectives range from an outright ban, to conditional access, and unrestrictive access, bringing into question the consequences of a market-driven objective of the introduction of individual tenure. Salient questions of an appropriate political structure include whether certain covenants should run with the land?[28] Another question: Is the relevant dispute settlement mechanism appropriate for resolving conflicts between individuals and their communities in the process of privatisation?

At the heart of the legislative enhancement of indigenous land tenure is an assumption of its communal character and linkage to a community. Even where individual land holding is permissible in an indigenous community, the existence of such a community is assumed. What is less clear is how an indigenous community is to be defined. Should such a community be defined by blood ancestry only or should other facts of association be in play. The idea that indigenous communities can be easily defined appears less so that they can be described or identified. At one end of the spectrum is what could be termed the 'traditional' sense of indigenous communities that inhabit a discernible physical and cultural space organised largely around blood ancestry. At the other end of the spectrum is the construction of indigenous communities in terms of associational facts beyond blood ancestry. These two spectrums, including the shades in between, are found in the legislative articulation of indigenous communities. For example, Kenya's Community Land Act 2016 defines a 'community' as 'a consciously distinct and organised group of users of community land who are citizens of Kenya and share any of the following attributes: common ancestry; similar culture or unique mode of livelihood; socio-economic or other similar common interest; geographical space; ecological space; or ethnicity'. The use of 'community' land in Kenyan legislation contemplates 'customary' land and therefore suggests that an indigenous community must be a customary community organised around common ancestry, unique culture, and ethnicity. The associational facts recognised by the CLA are more than those recognised by the

[26] See for example, Bhandar (2015).

[27] See for example, Claassens and Cousins (2008); Ubink and Amanor (2008).

[28] See for example, Burrows (2015), p. 91.

Constitution of Kenya 2010, which defined communities in terms of 'ethnicity, culture or similar community of interest'.[29]

Tanzania's Village Land Act 1999 defines a village as a village registered under the Local Government (District Authority) Act. The requirement for such a registration is that a prescribed number of households have settled in Mainland Tanzania. There are no expressed facts of association. Indeed, it could be surmised that all associational facts are contemplated, even though a village of blood ancestry is expected to be the most likely to be registered. The Ghana Land Act 2020 defines a community as a group of families and individuals living in a territorial area and that has common interests in areas of habitation, agriculture, communal land use and protection of land, whether cultivated or lying fallow, forests, places of cultural importance, such as pastures, and water sources.

The importance of an appropriate definition of an indigenous community stems from the fact that, by virtue of customary law, these communities are recognised in law as bearing rights and duties as defined by customary law. Indigenous land tenure is at the heart of the survival and identity of indigenous peoples. In turn, the identity of communities leads to an identification of members and non-members of the community. Non-members of the community are not entitled to customary land, leading to two related questions. The first is whether the identification of communities is easily facilitated by indigenous land tenure legislation.[30] The answer to this question lies in the requirement of the registration and representation of indigenous communities as a basis for the application of indigenous land tenure legislations, and the second is the rights of members and non-members of indigenous communities. Can they become members of these communities by choice and in furtherance of their right to a culture of their choice? To what extent can rights of freedom of movement and residence override the exclusion of non-members in a community?

These questions of belonging and exclusion have been at the core of land-related conflicts across Africa, including access to grazing lands in Nigeria and Kenya. The absence and neglect of access to indigenous lands in both countries has fuelled considerable controversy. One credible response is to formalise access to indigenous lands by non-members, even in light of constitutional rights of association and freedom of movement. An example is found in Kenya's Community Land Act, which formalises a process through which non-members may have access to grazing rights.[31]

The idea that the juristic personality of indigenous communities is 'granted' by indigenous land tenure legislation is not entirely correct but useful. Thus, many of the indigenous land tenure legislations craft a process for the recognition of indigenous communities. For example, the Kenyan CLA provides for a registration process for a community claiming a specific piece of land. The process is through an advertisement inviting members of the community to a meeting whose purpose is to

[29] Article 63(1) of the Kenyan Constitution.

[30] See generally Odote (2013), p. 97.

[31] See sect 28(3) of the CLA.

elect members of the Community Land Management Committee.[32] After such an election, the Committee lodges appropriate documents, which include the name of the community and the land to be registered.[33] After a survey of such land and a period of public comment, the community land is to be registered in a community land registry.[34] Until the land is registered, the title to the customary land shall vest in the relevant local government on behalf of the communities.[35]

A critical question is whether communal ownership is the defining characteristic of indigenous land tenure. Are there other characteristics such as state ownership and access rights? Emerging trends of legislative enhancement of indigenous tenure deliver a unanimous answer in recognising communal interests ranging from the vesting of the radical title in communities, such as in Ghana and Kenya, to rights of access and use, especially in the case of the eminent domain of African states, such as Tanzania. Clearly, what distinguishes indigenous land tenure is what the relevant land tenure legislation provides. Although the example of a radical title would be easier to understand, indigenous land-tenure user rights are not less clear. Norms developed by communities govern how members of a community interact with the recognised land tenure. This fact is evident where indigenous land tenure legislation recognises the customary law of the user community.

An often-forgotten feature of indigenous law crucial in reforming indigenous law is the configuration of the former's dispute-settlement process in the plural legal system. The challenge of plural legal systems is the configuration of these dispute settlement processes with the mainstream legal system. Should the legal system establish a dispute-settlement process for the other legal orders, or should the normal process through regular judicial hierarchies continue? Since different legal orders within a plural system continue with or without the sanction of the dominant legal order, it is often controversial whether the majority courts should accept the outcomes of the dispute settlement frameworks of inferior legal orders. Therefore, it is not surprising that it is urged that a key piece of statutory reform requires changes in norm-making and dispute-settlement processes. How these changes are reflected in the reform process is very important because it tests a commitment to protecting the inferior normative order. Since considerable blame is heaped on traditional hierarchies as responsible for the ills of customary law, it is often the case that changing these traditional hierarchies is an attractive proposition. However, how these changes could be implemented is not an easy task. In what ways, it may be asked, Should these traditional hierarchies be changed or reconstituted?

---

[32] See sect 7 (1)(2)(3) and (4) of the CLA.

[33] See sect 7 of the CLA.

[34] See sect 8 of the CLA.

[35] See sect 10(3) of the CLA.

5 The Catalytic Effect of the Regional and International Protection of Indigenous Property

The development of indigenous property has benefited from many regional and international articulations of understandings on indigenous property. A crucial part of these understandings is the recognition of the right to culture and collective rights which recognise the communal nature of indigenous property. In particular, the international Bill of Rights, the Universal Declaration of Human Rights (UDHR),[36] the International Covenant for Economic Social and Cultural Rights (ICESCR),[37] and the International Covenant on Civil and Political Rights (ICCPR)[38] recognise collective and group rights. The UDHR in Article 27 provides that everyone has the right freely to participate in the cultural life of the community, to enjoy the arts, and to share in scientific advancement and its benefits. Article 1(1) of the ICESCR provides that: 'All peoples have the right of self-determination. By virtue of that right they freely determine their political status and freely pursue their economic, social and cultural development'. Article 15 further recognises the right of everyone: (a) To take part in cultural life; (b) To enjoy the benefits of scientific progress and its applications; (c) To benefit from the protection of the moral and material interests resulting from any scientific, literary, or artistic production of which he is the author. Article 27 of the ICCPR provides that: 'In those States in which ethnic, religious or linguistic minorities exist, persons belonging to such minorities shall not be denied the right, in community with the other members of their group, to enjoy their own culture, to profess and practise their own religion, or to use their own language'. It appears clearly from the cast of the ICESCR and ICCPR that they protect group rights as in Article 1 of both treaties. On the other hand, Article 27 of the ICCPR and Article 15 of the ICESCR recognises the collective rights of individuals, in that they can exercise their rights in community with other persons.[39] Beyond the references to the right to culture, there is no specific reference to indigenous property, which is not fatal since clarifications of the group and collective rights to culture in these treaties influence and persuade African state parties in their conception, interpretation, and imagination of indigenous property. Similarly, there is little doubt that the United Nations Declaration of the Rights of Indigenous Peoples (DRIP)[40] will be of considerable persuasion to African courts in their articulation of indigenous property. In particular, the key provisions of the DRIP, for our purposes, are therefore important. Article 1 of the DRIP states that indigenous peoples have the right to the full enjoyment, as a collective or as individuals, of all human rights and fundamental freedoms as recognised in the Charter of the United Nations, the Universal Declaration of Human Rights, and international human rights law. The right to

[36] Hereafter UDHR.

[37] Hereafter ICESCR.

[38] Hereafter ICCPR.

[39] See Niec (1997).

[40] Hereafter DRIP. Forty-nine (49) African countries have signed the DRIP.

cultural and intellectual property is articulated in a number of ways. First in Article 11, paragraph 1 which provides that indigenous peoples have the right to practise and revitalise their cultural traditions and customs. This includes the right to maintain, protect, and develop the past, present, and future manifestations of their cultures, such as archaeological and historical sites, artefacts, designs, ceremonies, technologies, and visual and performing arts and literature. Paragraph 2 of Article 11 directs states to provide redress through effective mechanisms, which may include restitution, developed in conjunction with indigenous peoples, with respect to their cultural, intellectual, religious, and spiritual property taken without their free, prior, and informed consent or in violation of their laws, traditions, and customs. A second articulation can be found in Article 31(1) which provides that:

> Indigenous peoples have the right to maintain, control, protect and develop their cultural heritage, traditional knowledge and traditional cultural expressions, as well as the manifestations of their sciences, technologies and cultures, including human and genetic resources, seeds, medicines, knowledge of the properties of fauna and flora, oral traditions, literatures, designs, sports and traditional games and visual and performing arts. They also have the right to maintain, control, protect and develop their intellectual property over such cultural heritage, traditional knowledge, and traditional cultural expressions.

Again, Article 31(2) directs states, in conjunction with indigenous peoples, to take effective measures to recognise and protect the exercise of these rights.

The right to participation and consultation contained in Article 18 of the DRIP ensures that indigenous people have a fundamental input in how the state designs a protection model for their protection. Consequently, indigenous peoples have the right to participate in decision-making in matters which would affect their rights, through representatives chosen by themselves in accordance with their own procedures, as well as to maintain and develop their own indigenous decision-making institutions. Article 19 requires states to consult and cooperate in good faith with indigenous peoples concerned through their own representative institutions to obtain their free, prior, and informed consent before adopting and implementing legislative or administrative measures that may affect them. An important way in which indigenous people can participate in protecting their intellectual property is through their normative system. In this regard, Article 34 of DRIP provides that indigenous peoples have the right to promote, develop, and maintain their institutional structures and their distinctive customs, spirituality, traditions, procedures, practices, and, in the cases where they exist, juridical systems or customs, in accordance with international human rights standards.

Article 27 of DRIP encapsulates the objective of the human rights protection model. The said article provides that states shall establish and implement, in conjunction with the indigenous peoples concerned, a fair, independent, impartial, open, and transparent process, giving due recognition to indigenous peoples' laws, traditions, customs, and land tenure systems, to recognise and adjudicate the rights of indigenous peoples pertaining to their lands, territories, and resources, including those which were traditionally owned or otherwise occupied or used. Indigenous peoples have the right to participate in this process.

The rights of indigenous peoples are not absolute. Article 46 provides that indigenous people must exercise their rights in the context of the Charter of the United Nations and within the territorial integrity or political unity of sovereign and independent states. These limitations are limited to such limitations as are determined by law and in accordance with international human rights obligations. Any such limitations shall be non-discriminatory and strictly necessary solely for the purpose of securing due recognition and respect for the rights and freedoms of others and for meeting the just and most compelling requirements of a democratic society.

On a regional basis, The African Charter on Human and Peoples' Rights also makes provisions for collective and group cultural rights. Article 17(2) of the Charter provides that every person shall freely take part in the cultural life of their community. Article 22 of the Charter further provides that all peoples shall have the right to their economic, social, and cultural development with due regard to their freedom and identity and in the equal enjoyment of the common heritage of mankind. To strengthen the rights of groups to cultural development, Article 18(3) provides that states are to promote and protect morals and traditional values recognised by the community. It is beyond doubt that the African Charter truly recognises group rights to culture in addition to recognising the individual right to culture. Case law such as *Centre for Minority Rights Development v Endorois Community v Kenya*[41] and *African Commission on Human and Peoples' Rights v Republic of Kenya*[42] emanating from the African Court on Human and Peoples Rights, and based largely on the ACHPR, support this conclusion.

6 Conclusion

It is difficult not to conclude that the nature of indigenous property and indigenous laws presents a considerable challenge in any process of development of indigenous land tenure in an African state. The fact that more than 3000 ethnic groups in Africa speak more than 2100 languages, observing indigenous law in a continent of 53 states that are underdeveloped and developing, beset with significant political, socio-economic, and governance crises; making up over 90% of an estimated population of 1.2 billion people, with roughly half of this population living in urban areas; with a land mass 30.37 million square kilometres—60% of which is estimated to be subject to indigenous land tenure and thus subject to the management of indigenous communities—is proof of this challenge. Even though this book argues that the legislative reform of indigenous land tenure generally bodes well for African states, the rest of this book recognises the enormous challenges that confine this conclusion.

[41] [2009] ACPHR 102.

[42] Application No 006/2012.

References

Allot A (1965a) The future of African law. In: Kuper H, Kuper L (eds) African law: adaptation and development. University of California Press, Berkeley
Allot A (1965b) Towards the unification of laws in Africa. Int Comp Law Q 14:366
Allot A (1977) The people as law-makers: custom, practice, and public opinion as sources of law in Africa and England. J Afr Law 21:1–23
Allot A (1985) Customary law: its place and meaning in contemporary African legal systems. J Afr Law 9:82
Bennett TW (1995) Human rights and African customary law. Juta, Cape Town
Bennett TW (2004) Customary law in Africa. Juta, Cape Town
Bennett TW (2009) Re-introducing African customary law to the South African legal system. Am J Comp Law 57:1–31
Bhandar B (2015) Status as property: identity, land and the dispossession of first nation women in Canada. In: Bhandar B, Bhandar D (eds) Reflections on dispossession: critical feminisms. Living Commons Press, London
Burrows J (2015) Aboriginal title and private property. SCLR 7:91
Chanock M (1985) Law custom and social change: the colonial experience in Malawi and Zambia. Cambridge University Press, London
Chanock M (1991) A peculiar sharpness: an essay on property in the history of customary law in colonial Africa. J Afr Hist 32(1):65–88
Chanock M (2001) The making of South African legal culture 1902–1936: fear, favour and prejudice. Cambridge University Press, London
Chimhowu A (2019) The 'new' African customary land tenure: characteristic, features and policy implications of a new paradigm. Land Use Policy 81:897
Claassens A, Cousins B (eds) (2008) Land power and custom; controversies generated by South Africa's Communal Land Rights Act. UCT Press, Cape Town
Cotula L (ed) (2007) Changes in 'customary' land tenure systems in Africa. IIED
Diala A (2021) Legal pluralism and the future of personal family laws in Africa. Int J Law Policy Family 35:1–17
Elias TO (1956) The nature of African customary law. Manchester University Press, London
Fenrich J, Galizzi P, Higgins T (eds) (2013) The future of African customary law. Cambridge University Press, London
Kerr AJ (2009) The nature and future of customary law. SALJ:677–689
Knight R (2010) Statutory recognition of customary land rights in Africa: an investigation into best practices for law making and implementation. FAO
Knoetze E, Olivier M (2005) To develop or not to develop the customary law: that is the question in Bhe. Obiter 26:126–132
McAuslan P (2015) Property and empire: from colonialism to globalisation and back. Soc Leg Stud 24(3):339–357. https://doi.org/10.1177/0964663915593010
Mqeke R (2009) Guidelines for determining the constitutional injunction to apply customary law in the new South Africa. South Afr Law J 126:689
Niec H (1997) Cultural rights: at the end of the world decade for cultural development at www.dba.es/cerc/interaccio2002/seminar/s6/docu10.htm. Accessed 25 August 2009
Odote C (2013) The dawn of Uhuru? implications of the constitutional recognition of communal land rights in pastoral areas of Kenya. Nomadic Peoples 17(1):87–105, 97
Rautenbach C (1999) A Commentary on the application of the Bill of Rights to customary law. Obiter 20:113–132
Snyder F (1981) Colonialism and legal form: the creation of 'customary law' in Senegal. J Leg Plur Unoff Law 19:49
Ubink JM, Amanor K (eds) (2008) Contesting land and custom in Ghana: state chief and the citizen. Leiden University Press, Leiden

Wily LA (2011) 'The law is to blame': the vulnerable status of common property rights in Sub-Saharan Africa. Dev Change 42(3):733. https://doi.org/10.1111/j.1467-7660.2011.01712.x
Wily L (2012) Customary land tenure in the modern world. Rights and Resources Initiative, Washington DC
Woodman GR (1969) Some realism about customary law – the West African experience. Wisconsin Law Rev:128–152
Woodman GR (1985) Customary law, state courts, and the notion of institutionalization of norms in Ghana and Nigeria. In: Allott A, Woodman GR (eds) People's law and state law: the Bellagio Papers. Eons, Dordrecht, pp 143–163
Woodman GR (1988) How state courts create customary law in Ghana and Nigeria. In: Morse BW, Woodman GR (eds) Indigenous law and the state. Fans, Dordrecht, pp 181–220
Woodman GR (1995) European influence on land law and land use in colonial Ghana and Nigeria. In: De Moor J, Rothermund D (eds) Our laws, their lands: land laws and land use in modern colonial societies. LIT, Westview, Münster and Hamburg, pp 5–24
Woodman GR (1996) Customary land law in the Ghanaian courts. Ghana University Press, Accra
Woodman GR (2001) Customary law in common law systems. IDS Bull 32:28–34

An Overview of Indigenous Land Tenure in Africa

Contents

1 Introduction 19
2 Communal Ownership and Management of Indigenous Land Tenure 20
3 Access and Secondary Rights in Indigenous Land Tenure 23
4 Marginalised Stakeholders and Access to Indigenous Land Tenure 24
5 The Oral and Undocumented Nature of Indigenous Land Tenure 25
6 The Sacred Nature of Indigenous Land Tenure 26
7 A Longitudinal Overview of the Privatisation of Indigenous Land Tenure in Africa 26
8 Conclusion 30
References 31

1 Introduction

This chapter provides an overview of the nature of indigenous land tenure as a context for an evaluation of the privatisation of indigenous land tenure and its effect on the future of indigenous law in Africa. It is taken for granted, as demonstrated in the first chapter, that indigenous land tenure is part of, if not the principal example of, a constitutional indigenous property. An appropriate normative framework for indigenous property is crucial in constructing a sustainable framework that meaningfully and substantively reconciles the exercise and objectives of individual land tenure within a communal property framework in Africa. Chapter "The Privatisation of Indigenous Land Tenure Development and the Future of African Indigenous Law" examined the nature and features of indigenous law in Africa to establish the context for the statutory reform of indigenous property, dwelling on the features that would frame and impact the privatisation of indigenous land tenure. As stated above, this chapter relates how the general features of indigenous law in Africa inform and impact the privatisation of indigenous land tenure, which informs a forecast of the future of indigenous law in Africa. Since privatisation contemplates individual control, use, and sometimes title to indigenous land tenure, it is often the excision of land from communal indigenous land tenure. Privatisation can be said to support

E. Nwauche, *The Privatisation of Indigenous Land Tenure and the Future of African Indigenous Law*, https://doi.org/10.1007/978-3-032-14881-0_2

community members and citizens to enjoy the benefits of communal land tenure, allowing members of indigenous communities to use their entitlements, to act as a bulwark against state power[1] and effectively participate in national economies.[2] The fact that indigenous land tenure consists of more than 60% of land in Africa suggests the enormous significance of indigenous land tenure, and legislative plans to alter some of its fundamental foundations have significant consequences for the future of indigenous law, whether the reform process succeeds or fails. As stated in chapter "The Privatisation of Indigenous Land Tenure Development and the Future of African Indigenous Law", the remains of indigenous law after privatisation are the focus of this book. While chapter "The Privatisation of Indigenous Land Tenure Development and the Future of African Indigenous Law" examined the broad features of indigenous law, this chapter concentrates on the features of indigenous land tenure and how they impact the privatisation. To accomplish this task, what follows is a consideration of communal ownership and management of indigenous land tenure. The question of access to indigenous land tenure and secondary rights is considered next. How marginalised stakeholders in indigenous land tenure fare in a privatisation process follows. The oral nature of indigenous land tenure and the attendant consequences that indigenous land tenure is undocumented is the fourth feature considered. The sacred nature of indigenous land tenure is examined, and a longitudinal overview of privatisation forms the final part of this chapter.

2 Communal Ownership and Management of Indigenous Land Tenure

Indigenous land tenure is the material foundation of indigenous peoples in all ramifications and is at the centre of the social, religious, economic, and political life in these communities, and it is important to constantly interrogate this question. Due to the agrarian nature of African communities, land is the most important form of family property because it provides a means of subsistence, is of sacerdotal importance, is a store of wealth, and therefore is of great social and economic significance. It is therefore important that, to sustain the community, its property must be protected and should remain as much as possible within the community.

Since the distinguishing feature of indigenous land tenure is communal ownership and/or management of land tenure, all development of indigenous land tenure must grapple with different dimensions of this challenge. Communal ownership of indigenous land tenure is expressed in different forms and styles, but generally through traditional authorities of the community and the family. Like all societies, indigenous communities struggle over how to express their autonomy. For example, even in circumstances where the radical title to indigenous land tenure is vested in

[1] Locke and Macpherson (1980), p. 124; Ellickson (1993), p. 1315.

[2] See for example, Flanagan and Alcantara (2002).

the post-colonial African state, some powers of management are granted to indigenous communities that are implicitly or expressly exercised by traditional authorities who develop expertise in the management of indigenous land tenure. It is therefore important to ensure that the views of indigenous communities are recognised in a reform process. 'Although several African states have appointed reform commissions to contextualise and articulate the public participation process aimed at guiding legislatures, the question remains whether these commissions have included specific inquiries targeted for indigenous land reform'.

While it is true that representatives of indigenous communities are members of legislative houses, it appears a matter for serious consideration whether indigenous communities are specifically consulted in the process of development. Available evidence is mixed, but it largely suggests that indigenous communities have not been adequately consulted through the reform process. Whether the development efforts in several states would have been different had these consultations taken place is an open question but it ought to be remembered that indigenous land tenure is a product of the relationships fostered by indigenous norms. A top-down approach that characterises the reform process has missed some of these norms that could provide a context in which the privatisation of indigenous land tenure can thrive.

Another challenge of the development process is how to infuse multi-stakeholder participation in indigenous governance as a governance entity separate from or including traditional authorities. Appropriate questions include the representation of stakeholders and whether they can outvote traditional authorities or other members. Another option is to establish separate entities that operate independently from traditional authorities, who could then take on an advisory role while the daily management is handled by this committee.

Yet, another challenge is the role of families within indigenous communities. In several states, families are the operational arm of communities, often holding indigenous land tenure with other traditional authorities. In recognition of the importance of families to African states, the African Charter on Human and Peoples' Rights makes elaborate provisions, including the preamble to the Charter that urges member- states to take 'into consideration the virtues of their historical traditions and values of African civilization which should inspire and characterize their reflection on the concept of human and peoples' rights'. The Charter further declares in Article 18(1) that the family shall be the natural unit and basis of society and shall be protected by the state, which shall take care of its physical and moral health. In Article 18(2), the charter places a duty on state parties to assist the family, as the custodian of morals and traditional values recognised by the community. The charter also recognises the duties owed by members of the family. Article 27(1) provides that 'every individual shall have duties towards his family and society'. These duties are further elucidated in Article 29(1) which states that an individual shall have the duty: 'to preserve the harmonious development of the family and to work for the cohesion and respect of the family; to respect his parents at all times, to maintain them in case of need'. The 'cohesion and respect' of the family can be easily tied to indigenous land tenure, which has developed norms that protect the relationships nurtured by it. The provisions of the charter are an affirmation of a fundamental ordering of African communities and, indeed, all communities. African families act as units of cohesion, solidarity, and culturalisation, serving moral, economic, social, cultural, and political purposes. Therefore, to sustain indigenous communities, family tenurial relationships should be protected and remain as much as possible within the family. The norms created by pre-colonial African communities to preserve family property lay essentially in the fact that living family members automatically inherited family and communal property as a matter of law. Another principle for preserving family land is that the land was also inalienable, ensuring that family property was preserved for generations. The advent of colonialism and the post-colonial African state has led to an amelioration of this rule as noted above. Privatisation poses serious problems for African families because of the impact on the relationships that indigenous land tenure supports and nurtures. The inalienability and automatic inheritance of family property face a fundamental challenge when individuals, under their right to constitutional property or for other reasons, assert that family property should migrate to individual ownership. In many ways, this is possible. First, family property can be sold by members of the family, as pointed out above. Second, it may also be the subject of a gift. Third, family property may be partitioned, bringing the family property to an end. Partitioning can a decision by family members, and it can also be by order of a court of law. For the latter, where some family members are denied participation in the family property, and it appears that the relationship *inter se* has broken down irretrievably, a court could order partition and even the sale of family property. As stated above, there are numerous instances in which family property is terminated which supports the conclusion that because of the liberal ethos of the post-colonial African state, individual ownership of family property is often encouraged at the expense of family and communal ownership.

The utility of family land is determined by the benefits that its nature brings to its members. The family property provides a residence for its members. It enables members to share in the economic proceeds of managing family property, acting as a social net for less fortunate members. In the case of land, it ensures the availability of food. The property of the family encourages the continuous interaction of its members, which is critical to the growth of society. It enhances the values of solidarity with others and cultivates an ethic of caring for others. Finally, the common involvement in its protection and management underlies the duties members owe to a collective whose protection is vital for their survival.

Dispute settlement within family and community hierarchies is crucial for sustaining the family and community. Collectively described as alternative dispute resolution, indigenous authorities have for centuries developed an excellent ability to manage and settle disputes that are often oral and generally outside the purview of state law,[3] and from time to time, these outcomes are brought to state courts that have recognised the validity of these mechanisms. When that occurs, considerable

[3] See, for example, the following representative literature. Igbokwe (1997), p. 201; Elombi (1993), p. 803; Allott (1988); Ikeyi and Maduka (2014), pp. 328–349; Koblaive and Nyinevi (2019), pp. 587–607; Kariuki and Nwauche (2023), pp. 70–83.

issues arise from the plural character of African legal systems and their subordination to indigenous legal orders. State courts can negate carefully negotiated tenure norms and principles that have developed even in the aftermath of the statutory development of indigenous land tenure. State courts are not under an obligation to adhere to a constitutionalised indigenous property system that begins from indigenous laws that are not readily applicable before them. Although a few states like South Africa and Kenya have constitutionalised indigenous laws as equal to common and civil law, there is widespread propensity to imagine indigenous tenure as analogous to state tenure because of privatisation. State courts that are faced with adjudicating indigenous land disputes readily turn to common and civil law principles rather than indigenous law principles that are often difficult to ascertain.

Indigenous communities struggle to contain the state's power to forcefully acquire indigenous land tenure. States that quickly expropriate the tenure of indigenous land suggest inadequate respect for indigenous land tenure. The link between compulsory acquisition of indigenous land tenure and privatisation appears tenuous but it can be explained by the potential use of the power of compulsory acquisition to promote the latter. A state that readily expropriates indigenous land tenure could be characterised as breaching the constitutional value of appropriate recognition of indigenous land tenure.

In all, the extent to which African states recognise aspects of communal ownership and management in their articulation of a constitutionalised indigenous property, discussed in chapter "The Privatisation of Indigenous Land Tenure Development and the Future of African Indigenous Law", is important to bear in mind. It is important to question whether the challenges of community ownership and management as part of a constitutional indigenous property and land tenure have informed the privatisation of indigenous land tenure. Much of how a constitutional vision of indigenous property can be realised depends on African judiciaries, which are obligated to uphold the principles of indigenous land tenure as they interpret the legislative development of indigenous land tenure.

3 Access and Secondary Rights in Indigenous Land Tenure

One of the unique features of indigenous land tenure is that the collective title supports multiple and interlocking secondary tenure rights on the same land. The communal ownership of indigenous land tenure also includes access rights for communal and family members. We conclude that indigenous land tenure is constitutional property and is even considered so in several African states. Whether the principles of constitutional property, which prioritises private interests in the balance between public and private interests, also applies to indigenous land tenure is debatable because of the communal and family ethos of indigenous land tenure. A clear vision of constitutionalised indigenous land tenure that privileges family and communal interests is crucial for a meaningful legislative reform of indigenous land tenure. Unfortunately, privatisation of indigenous land tenure in several states challenges these assumptions because privatisation, by its definition, is designed for individual benefit in many respects and in several states. Although there are nuances in the manner in which individual benefit is recognised in a communal setting, in some states, there is evidence, as explored in chapter "Models of Private Interests in Indigenous Land Tenure in Africa", that it is possible, suggesting an understanding of a constitutionalised indigenous land tenure that privileges the community. States with this vision of constitutionalised indigenous land tenure are under an obligation to continuously ensure the fidelity of the statutory development of indigenous land tenure to this vision.

The duties of communal and family leadership include ensuring that family and communal members have access to indigenous land tenure. These access rights ensured that all family members and foreigners who pay fees, such as pastoralists, achieved their objectives within communal and family oversight. Although these rights are secondary, they are crucial and interlinked to family and communal titles. A key challenge for indigenous land tenure is preserving these tenure rights. The sustainability of indigenous land tenure depends on the state and communal capacity to capture these secondary rights of value which include several temporary and seasonal access rights, informal collateral transactions, sub-leases, and possessory transactions. As the discussions of different indigenous tenure reforms show in chapter "Models of Private Interests in Indigenous Land Tenure in Africa", there is potential for securing secondary rights with appropriate imagination, where ownership and management of indigenous land tenure are vested in indigenous communities. It appears plausible to engraft these secondary rights on the privatised land tenure. A constitutionalised indigenous property framework requires African judiciaries to recognise secondary rights even where the legislature has failed to do so.

4 Marginalised Stakeholders and Access to Indigenous Land Tenure

Also important for indigenous communities is the commitment to ensure that the internal dynamics of traditional hierarchies and communities ensure broad-based stakeholder engagement, including fair and adequate gender representation. The hierarchical and patriarchal structure of indigenous law constructed several norms that marginalise and exclude women and other disadvantaged stakeholders from accessing indigenous land tenure. Inadequate mechanisms for redress perpetuated by patriarchy often mask exclusion with enlightened paternalism, where obligations of care by male hierarchy are assumed by indigenous law to be adequate for the less privileged, disempowered women, and other stakeholders.

All the statutory tenure development legislation which is analysed in the remainder of this book, especially in chapter "Patriarchy, Gender, and Access to Indigenous Land Tenure in Africa", affirms the rights of women to indigenous land tenure. Some of them mandate proportional women's representation. It is fitting that the momentum towards these changes has occurred outside the tenure development process across Africa, as several national courts have struck down discriminatory practices on the grounds of constitutionalised rights to equality and non-discrimination. These cases are discussed in chapter "Patriarchy, Gender, and Access to Indigenous Land Tenure in Africa" and highlight that tenure reform has reinforced the fact that indigenous laws in Africa can thrive without patriarchy.

The available evidence suggests a mixed outcome in ensuring adequate management of inadequate rules of access and grievance resolution and shows the need for a wholesome approach to integrating social practices in the tenure development process beyond legislative development. How states can ensure that social practices align with legislated access to indigenous land tenure for marginalised stakeholders will always be a challenge for indigenous land tenure. It is important to note that enhanced gender access to indigenous land tenure represents a fundamental achievement of the legislative development of indigenous land tenure because it challenges and puts to rest the idea that the socially constructed patriarchal foundations of indigenous land tenure are an immutable foundation of indigenous law in Africa. A constitutional indigenous land tenure recognises equal access, and this issue is discussed in chapter "Patriarchy, Gender, and Access to Indigenous Land Tenure in Africa".

5 The Oral and Undocumented Nature of Indigenous Land Tenure

Since indigenous land tenure is held orally and represented in many African states, there are inadequate and unreliable land records of primary and secondary rights in these communities. The widespread belief that orality is a fundamental tenet of indigenous laws in Africa is unsettling because it supports an unreal idea that the flexibility of indigenous law practices is rooted in the orality of indigenous law and that writing is foreign to indigenous law. Unfortunately, the statutory reform process has been conducted in several African countries with inadequate land records. What would have been a precursor to privatisation was adequate land records. Decades after the commencement of systematic privatisation, several African countries have inadequate land tenure records. Adequate documentation enables indigenous communities to protect their interests in the privatisation process.

It is therefore easy to imagine the considerable difficulties when privatisation results in documentary outcomes and distorts the capacity of indigenous communities to manage the excision of parts of their tenure for their members. The maintenance of secondary rights in indigenous land tenure can thrive better when there is documentation of indigenous land tenure.

Indeed, the development process has highlighted the obligations of land management bodies to record their land tenure. The option of readily available low-cost technologies is available for indigenous communities to assist them in the registration, recognition, and use of privatised land tenure. This issue is discussed in chapter "Documentation and Registration of Indigenous Land Tenure".

6 The Sacred Nature of Indigenous Land Tenure

Across Africa, indigenous land was considered as sacred,[4] understood as the setting aside of something important,[5] and several African communities worshipped the land and its constructs as deities, representing the special and unique standing of land in the lives of indigenous peoples.[6] Ancestral worship is often regarded as a pillar of African indigenous religion[7] and is directly constructed around land, which is believed to be owned by the living and the dead. Ancestral worship was important for many indigenous communities because ancestors buried on the land protected the living and, in return, required care in the way they were treated and in the lives of members of the community. Alienation of such sacred land without communal sanction is regarded sacrilege. Decades of colonial rule, including the growth of the Abrahamic religions—Islam and Christianity—have weakened the sacred nature of indigenous land and customs emanating from such sacrality. Recognising the sacred nature of indigenous land tenure as part of acceptable practices, duties, and obligations in the privatisation of indigenous land tenure seems a distant possibility, but underscores the unique character of indigenous land tenure and its relational ethic of solidarity, compassion, care, and responsibility. Unfortunately, this feature of indigenous land tenure is not of much significance, if at all. There is a difficulty in factoring in the sacred in a very secular process. Perhaps respect for the dignity and survival of the community in the process of privatisation could be one way.

7 A Longitudinal Overview of the Privatisation of Indigenous Land Tenure in Africa

Recognising individual interests in indigenous land tenure appears to be an inevitable process and, in a sense, recognises practices that are not entirely alien to indigenous communities in Africa. Although it is agreed that land as an economic and social resource can support individual and communal tenure, global trends show a preference for individual rather than communal land tenure as catalytic for

[4] See for example, Muhando (2005); Bakulumpagi (2021), pp. 305–327; Shipton (1994), pp. 347–377.

[5] See for example, Chidester (2011), pp. 84–90.

[6] See for example, Opata and Asogwa (2017), pp. 1–11; Sinthumule (2025); Kokou et al. (2008), pp. 158–169; Metcalfe et al. (2010), pp. 118–123.

[7] See for example, Obi (1963), p. 25; Allott(1966), pp. 139–143; Kludze (1973), pp. 105–107; Asante (1975), p. ch. 1. Fortes (2009), pp. 66–83; Reddy (2022), pp. 235–248.

development.[8] While it is generally believed that Hayekian economists led by De Soto heralded the privatisation of communal property for market access, poverty alleviation, and development, centuries of capitalist and colonial pressures in Africa have altered indigenous property relations to firmly recognise some form or another of the privatisation of indigenous land tenure. However, systematic privatisation of communal land tenure is of recent vintage,[9] and it is fair to argue that Africa is a good example of systematic and organised regional privatisation of communal land tenure that began in the late 1990s.[10]

It should not be surprising that individual interests existed with what is commonly characterised as communal indigenous land tenure in pre-colonial Africa, which can be described as the first stage of the privatisation of indigenous land tenure. Several pieces of evidence demonstrate that individual land tenure was part of African kingdoms, empires and communities. For example, Isaac Samuel writes of several private land holdings in pre-colonial Senegal, Mali, Nigeria, Sudan, and Ethiopia.[11] In pre-colonial Africa, in many African indigenous communities, land was the property of the community or traditional authorities in states with centralised authorities or monarchs. Members of the community enjoyed usufructuary or beneficial use rights. Indeed, many commentators have pointed to the possibility that individual land ownership was possible in some precolonial indigenous communities, which appears to be an exception rather than the rule.[12] The rights of possession enjoyed by families and rarely by members of indigenous communities were secure for limited periods to the exclusion of other members of the family and community. The heads of the family and the senior male figures of the family periodically supervised the allocation of family land to members. Alienation was possible to some extent, especially to other families and community members, as consideration for other valuable resources and services, and possibly limited to improvements on the land. Contrary to the romantic picture of functional indigenous land tenure systems, many of these communities were dysfunctional, often exhibiting the power asymmetries of communities defined by status and patriarchy. However, the system worked in many ways, anchored on access to land as a cornerstone of the socially constructed indigenous land tenure systems. Although this serves as a mere summary of the complex, interlocking, flexible, and contextual indigenous land tenure systems in different indigenous communities, it is enough to understand how the privatisation of indigenous land tenure has moved from access to ownership and exclusivity.

History does not support the idea that land tenure in pre-colonial Africa was entirely communal.

---

[8] See for example, De Soto (2000).

[9] See for example, Ely Jr. (2008); Rose (1996), p. 329.

[10] See for example, Oketh-Ogendo (2002); Knight (2010); Wily (2011), p. 733; Cotula (2007).

[11] See Samuel (2021).

[12] See, for example, Elias (1951, reprinted in 2024); Ollenu (1962).

The second stage of privatisation represents the early stages of colonialism to the end of colonial rule in the late 1950s and 1960s. The principal feature of this period is the objective of the colonial executive, legislature, and judiciary to diminish the impact of indigenous land tenure in response to internal and external forces. While members of indigenous communities sought to use land tenure as a source of value in the market economy introduced by the colonial government, colonial governments found indigenous land tenure strange and unlike individual exclusive ownership patterns of European land tenure.[13] Their response to pressures from commercial farmers and mining corporations to extract value from the colonial enterprise led to serious opposition to indigenous land tenure. These commercial and industrial interests sought ownership of vast tracts of land as part of their trading stock, which led to purchases from indigenous communities and allocations from the colonial government. It was the colonial judiciary that further entrenched the alienation of indigenous land tenure, which was often the consequence of privatisation. For example, in *Yesufu Esan v Bankole*[14] the West African Court of Appeal recognised a sale of family land, albeit with the consent of principal family members. Generally, the colonial judiciary recognised an evolving principle of indigenous law that had shifted from an outright sale of family land to the plausibility of conditional sales of family land due to the pressures of commercial agriculture, housing, and banking services.[15] These banking services arose from the use of family land as collateral for loans in many urbanised parts of colonial Africa in demand for commercial value. There is little doubt that there was widespread recognition of the threat of alienation to the concept of family land.[16]

Further threats to family property emerged in conveyancing practices where families wanting better terms have been conveying land held under customary tenure as 'estates in fee simple'.[17] In Ghana, cases such as *Lokko v Konklol*,[18] *Sam v Them*,[19] and *Kodadja v Tekpo*[20] all held that long uninterrupted occupation by a stool subject transformed usufructuary interests into interests that could be alienated or mortgaged, and was thus averse to the ownership of Ghanaian monarchs. In *Lokko*, the property was pledged and in *Sam*, the 'new' interest enabled resistance to attached the land for the Monarch's debt since the land had become his own due to the commercial farming he had undertaken on the land. Whether the usufructuary rights of a community member transferred from another member of the community

[13] See for example Asante (1975).

[14] (1951), p. 13 WACA 135; Adu-Gyamfi et al. (2020), pp. 163–181.

[15] See the following Lloyd (1960), pp. 11–20.

[16] See for example, Coker (1958).

[17] See Lloyd (1959), pp. 105–115.

[18] [1907] Res, 450.

[19] [1924] Sel. J. Div. Ct Gold Coast '21-25 (D. Ct.), p. 63.

[20] [1931] Sel. J. Div. Ct. Gold Coast '29-31 (C. Ct), p. 45.

or a stranger without the community's consent was settled by the time Ghana became independent is not clear.[21]

The pressures of commercialisation and cultural ideas about individual autonomy over indigenous land tenure in East Africa are similar to the experience of West Africa. Sales of indigenous land tenure were recognised in Kenya. Fiona Mackenzie, quoting records of Kenyan colonial administration, points out that in the late 1940s this administration favoured individual control as economically, agriculturally, and socially viable.[22] What compounded the tenure of indigenous land in colonial Africa was that there was little or no evidence of communal ownership of the tenure of indigenous land, which opened large tracts of uncultivated and 'idle' land to state appropriation. Consequently, colonial expropriatory legislation empowered colonial governments to acquire land in the public interest. Examples include Uganda, where the 1897 Land Regulations empowered the Governor to grant certificates of occupancy for a maximum period of 21 years. The grantee was required to develop at least a quarter of the area granted by the end of the first five years. The Crown Lands Ordinance (cap. 117) permitted the sale of Crown land to private individuals as freehold.

Furthermore, individual interests in land were registrable in colonial land registries, effectively converting individual interests in indigenous land tenure into English-type 'fee simple' interests, effectively excluding such interests from incidents of indigenous land tenure. Such conveyances modelled forms of transfer of a common-law tenure, to pass usufructuary interests in indigenous land tenure and thereby convert the same to a common-law freehold, especially where the sold land is registered. In Uganda, the Registration of Titles Ordinance (cap. 123) made it obligatory to register all grants in fees or terms of years and rendered all unregistered transactions invalid. All a community member would do is seek registration of their interests, which turns indigenous tenure into a common law tenure. In many other African states, there was no registration of title legislation, making all unregistered land, including orally held communal and family land, precarious because it had to be proved as a fact by the tenor of land registrations. A general conclusion of the second stage of the privatisation of indigenous land tenure is that by the 1960s, when many African states became independent, communal and family ownership of indigenous land tenure waned across Africa, and private interests became a strong possibility in indigenous land tenure.

The third stage of the privatisation of indigenous land tenure occurred roughly between the mid-1950s and the third wave of constitutionalism in Africa in the late 1980s and 1990s, when many African states returned to constitutional democracies from military and civilian dictatorships. This period is generally characterised by enhanced state control, including nationalisation of land for national development. In this process, the privatisation of indigenous land tenure continued in many ways. First, enhanced state control weakened indigenous land tenure promoting private

[21] See for example, Woodman (1967), pp. 457–477.

[22] Mackenzie (1996), pp. 73, 62–77.

interests in land. It was an era of state-led development designed to ensure that citizens of African states could access indigenous land tenure without the constraints of indigenous communities and their constituent families. Some examples will illustrate. In Malawi, for example, Section 25 of the 1965 Land Law vested customary land in the people of Malawi and vested the same on the President in perpetuity. Although a Chief could authorise usufructuary rights, it was done under the supervision of the State. To further privatise indigenous land tenure, the Customary Land Development Act of 1967 permitted the allocation of indigenous land declared by the State Land Act as registrable. Zambia's Land (Conversion of Titles) Act of 1975 vested all Zambian land in the President of Zambia to be held in perpetuity for the benefit of all Zambians, converting all land into leaseholds. Nigeria followed in 1978 with the Land Use Act of 1978.[23]

In the fourth and ongoing stage of organised and systematic privatisation of indigenous land tenure, an ongoing question is the management of a process that is as old as Africa. Chapters "Models of Private Interests in Indigenous Land Tenure in Africa" to "Arbitration and Adjudication of Indigenous Land Tenure Disputes" of this book discuss the ongoing privatisation of indigenous land tenure, drawing useful lessons in appropriate places. In addition, this section is closely related to chapter "The Privatisation of Indigenous Land Tenure Development and the Future of African Indigenous Law", which discusses the constant flux and development of indigenous law. If the privatisation of indigenous land tenure is as old as Africa, it is important to turn to a nuanced interpretation of such a process for a deeper contextual understanding. Such an interpretation enables the rejection of propositions that outright claim that privatisation is antithetical to indigenous land tenure.

8 Conclusion

The discussion of the features of indigenous land tenure in this chapter is intended to complement the broad discussion of the features of indigenous law and property in chapter "The Privatisation of Indigenous Land Tenure Development and the Future of African Indigenous Law". In this regard, the features of indigenous land tenure were aligned with the discussions of the features of indigenous law. This alignment enables us to forecast the future of indigenous law in Africa. It is plausible to argue that examining different perspectives on the features of indigenous land tenure could support the argument that privatisation, if undertaken within a constitutional indigenous property that recognises the communal ownership of indigenous tenure that ensures secondary rights and ensures gender access to indigenous land tenure in a written framework, bodes well for indigenous communities and fosters a progressive future for indigenous law in Africa. How African states have managed the framework set out above is the subject of the rest of this book.

[23] See for example Agbosu (1988), pp. 1–43.

References

Adu-Gyamfi S, Bempong E, Yartey HT, Darkwa BD (2020) British land policies in the Gold Coast and her relations with Asante. Studia Historiae Oeconomicae 38:163–181. https://doi.org/10.2478/sho-2020-0007

Agbosu LK (1988) The land use act and the state of Nigerian law. J Afr Law 32:1–43

Allott AN (1966) The Ashanti law of property. Ferdinand Enke Verlag, Stuttgart, pp 139–143

Allott AN (1988) Customary arbitrations in Nigeria: a comment on Agu v Ikewibe. J Afr Law 42

Asante SKB (1975) Property law and social goals in Ghana 1844–1966. Ghana Universities Press, Accra, ch 1

Bakulumpagi K (2021) Resolution of the African Commission on Human and Peoples' Rights on the protection of sacred natural sites and territories: a critical overview. Afr Human Rights Yearb 5:305–327. https://doi.org/10.29053/2523-1367/2021/v5a14

Chidester D (2011) Sacred. Mater Relig 7:84–90

Coker GBA (1958) Family property among the Yoruba. Sweet & Maxwell, London

Cotula L (ed) (2007) Changes in 'customary' land tenure systems in Africa. IIED

De Soto H (2000) The mystery of capital: why capitalism triumphs in the west and fails everywhere else. Transworld Digital, London

Elias TO (1951, reprinted in 2024) Nigerian law and custom. Routledge Revivals, UK

Ellickson R (1993) Property in land. Yale Law J 102:1315

Elombi G (1993) Customary arbitration: a Ghanaian trend reversed in Nigeria. Afr J Int Comp Law 5:803

Ely JW Jr (2008) The guardian of every other right: a constitutional history of property rights, 3rd edn. Oxford University Press, Oxford, p 26

Flanagan T, Alcantara C (2002) Individual property rights on Canadian reserves. The Fraser Institute Occasional Paper 15:60

Fortes M (2009) Ancestor worship in Africa in religion, morality and the person essays on Tallensi religion. Cambridge University Press, Cambridge, pp 66–83. https://doi.org/10.1017/CBO9780511557996.005

Igbokwe V (1997) The law and practice of customary arbitration: Agu v Ikewibe and applicable issues revisited. J Afr Law 41:201

Ikeyi N, Maduka T (2014) The binding effect of a customary arbitration award: exorcising the ghost of Agu v Ikewibe. J Afr Law 58:328–349

Kariuki F, Nwauche ES (2023) Reflections on the autonomous alternative justice system institutions in Kenya's alternative justice systems policy frameworks. Law Afr 1:70–83

Kludze APK (1973) Ewe law of property. Sweet & Maxwell, London, pp 105–107

Knight R (2010) Statutory recognition of customary land rights in Africa: an investigation into best practices for law making and implementation. FAO

Koblaive B, Nyinevi C (2019) A review of the legislative reform of customary arbitration in Ghana. Commonw Law Bull 45:587–607

Kokou K, Adjossou K, Kokutse AD (2008) Considering sacred and riverside forests in criteria and indicators of forest management in low wood producing countries: the case of Togo. Ecol Indicat 8(2):158–169

Lloyd PC (1959) Family property among the Yoruba. J Afr Law 3:105–115

Lloyd PC (1960) Some modern developments in Yoruba customary land law. J Afr Adm 12:11–20

Locke J, Macpherson CB (1980) Second treatise on government. Hackett Publishing Company, Indianapolis, p 124

Mackenzie F (1996) Conflicting claims to custom: land and law in Central Province, Kenya, 1915-52. J Afr Law 40(1):73, 62–77

Metcalfe K, French-Constant R, Gordon I (2010) Sacred sites as hotspots for biodiversity: the Three Sisters Cave complex in coastal Kenya. Oryx 44(1):118–123

Muhando J (2005) Scared sites and environmental conservation: a case study of Kenya. Indlinga Afr J Indigen Knowl Syst 4(2) https://hdl.handle.net/10520/EJC61476

Obi SN (1963) Ibo law of property. Butterworths, London, p 25
Oketh-Ogendo HWO (2002) The tragic African commons: a century of expropriation, suppression and subversion. Programme for Land and Agrarian Studies, University of the Western Cape
Ollenu NA (1962) Principles of customary land law in Ghana. Sweet & Maxwell, London
Opata CC, Asogwa O (2017) Title, rituals, and land use: the heritage of a Nigerian society. SAGE Open, pp 1–11 https://doi.org/10.1177/21582440166891
Reddy CS (2022) Ancestor cult and its significance in agricultural activities of Doko community of Gamo High Lands of Ethiopia. Man Environ Soc 3(2):235–248. https://doi.org/10.47509/MES.2022.v03i02.01
Rose CM (1996) Property as the keystone right? Notre Dame Law Rev 71:329
Samuel I (2021) Land and property in pre-colonial Africa: land ownership, land sales and the shortfalls of the 'land abundant Africa'. Afr Hist Extra https://www.africanhistoryextra.com/p/land-and-property-in-pre-colonial. Accessed 7 October 2025
Shipton P (1994) Land and culture in tropical Africa: soils symbols and the metaphysics of the mundane. Ann Rev Anthropol 23:347–377
Sinthumule NI (2025) Sacred natural sites as other effective area-based conservation measures (OECMS) for biodiversity conservation in South Africa: Key opportunities and challenges for policy and practice. J Nature Conserv 86:126935. https://doi.org/10.1016/j.jnc.2025.126935
Wily LA (2011) 'The law is to blame': the vulnerable status of common property rights in Sub-Saharan Africa. Dev Change 42(3):733. https://doi.org/10.1111/j.1467-7660.2011.01712.x
Woodman G (1967) The scheme of subordinate tenures to land in Ghana. Am J Comp Law 15(3):457–477

Models of Private Interests in Indigenous Land Tenure in Africa

Contents

1 Introduction 33
2 Private Interests in Communally Indigenous Land Tenure 34
2.1 Ghana 34
2.2 Kenya 39
2.3 Uganda 45
2.4 South Africa 49
2.5 Liberia 54
2.6 Sierra Leone 56
2.7 Tanzania 57
3 State Ownership and Privatised Indigenous Land Tenure 59
3.1 Mozambique 59
3.2 Angola 60
3.3 Nigeria 61
3.4 Botswana 64
3.5 Namibia 67
3.6 Ethiopia 68
3.7 Zimbabwe 73
4 An Assessment of the Future of Indigenous Law in Africa through the Models of Privatisation of Indigenous Land Tenure in Africa 77
5 Conclusion 81
References 82

1 Introduction

This chapter evaluates existing legislative frameworks for privatising indigenous land tenure in Africa, building on the context explored in chapters "The Privatisation of Indigenous Land Tenure Development and the Future of African Indigenous Law" and "An Overview of Indigenous Land Tenure in Africa" for reforming indigenous law, the importance of indigenous property, a constitutional vision for indigenous land tenure, and the features of indigenous land tenure.

E. Nwauche, *The Privatisation of Indigenous Land Tenure and the Future of African Indigenous Law*, https://doi.org/10.1007/978-3-032-14881-0_3

This chapter explores the impact of privatisation on indigenous land tenure in relation to indigenous law. Has privatisation changed indigenous law, and if so, what is the character of the 'new' indigenous law? Has indigenous law simply absorbed and adapted to change as it usually does? To answer this question, this chapter proceeds through an overview of the privatisation of indigenous land tenure under two broad headings. In the first group are countries like Ghana, Kenya, Uganda, South Africa, Tanzania, Liberia, and Sierra Leone, where indigenous land tenure is recognised as communally owned, even if it is managed by the state in differing proportions. In the second group of countries, indigenous land tenure as state property with differing forms of indigenous land tenure that should have disappeared with nationalisation of land, like in Mozambique, Angola, Nigeria, Botswana, Namibia, Ethiopia, and Zimbabwe, is explored. What are the implications of the survival of indigenous land tenure in these countries in the onslaught of privatisation of indigenous land tenure?

It is important to reiterate that these two categories are for analytical purposes to bring some understanding to the subject. Several states featured in each category can conveniently feature in the other category. The categories that appear below are not exhaustive but an attempt to make meaning of different iterations of privatised indigenous land tenure in Africa.

2 Private Interests in Communally Indigenous Land Tenure

The first category consists of countries whose constitutional and legislative framework recognises the privatisation of indigenous tenure within a communal indigenous land tenure framework.

2.1 Ghana

Ghana has more than 70 native ethnic groups, including the Akan, the Mole-Dagbon, the Ewe, the Ga-Dangme, the Gurma, the Guan, the Grusi, the Mande, and others. Ghana covers an area of 238,583 km^2, of which 227,533 km^2 is its land mass. Estimates vary, but there is consensus that the dominant land use is agricultural, particularly in rural areas where indigenous tenurial arrangements are prevalent.[1] Ghana's urban population is roughly 59.2% of the total population, indicating that the rest of the country lives in rural areas where indigenous land tenure is prevalent.[2]

[1] See generally https://www.cia.gov/the-world-factbook/countries/ghana/. See also Asaaga and Hirons (2019).

[2] Ibid.

After decades of the protection of indigenous land tenure, which has increasingly recognised the individualisation of indigenous land tenure,[3] Ghana's Land Act 2020[4] recognises five types of indigenous land tenure, which are the allodial title; customary law freehold; an usufructuary interest; a leasehold; and a customary tenancy.

The customary freehold is the ultimate interest that can be held in the tenure of indigenous land [5] around which other interests can arise. It is (a) an absolute interest in land which is not subject to any proprietary obligations but is subject to the jurisdictional and cultural rights of the stool, skin, clan, or family which holds the allodial title;[6] (b) acquired when a person or group of persons, where the law permits, purchases land outright from the stool,[7] skin,[8] clan,[9] or family[10] which holds the allodial title or acquired by reason of gift or inheritance; and (c) of perpetual duration and is inheritable and alienable without the consent of or payment to the stool, skin, clan, or family. It is usual to imagine skin and stool[11] as well as clans and families[12] as holders of allodial titles to indigenous land tenure[13] that has now included private persons, although it is argued that the use of the phrase 'may have been acquired' indicates that relevant allodial titles are those in existence at the commencement of the GLA. Section 2 of the GLA provides that an individual could acquire allodial title through purchase, subject to obtaining the consent of the family and community and the National Council of Chiefs in respect to community land, in accordance with Section 267 of the 1992 Constitution.[14]

---

[3] See the following for an overview of customary land tenure in Ghana before the Ghana Land Act. Kasanga and Kotey (2001); Lambrecht and Asare (2016), pp. 251–263; Agbosu et al. (2007).

[4] Hereafter referred to as 'GLA'.

[5] For an overview of Ghanaian land tenure, see Bentsi-Enchill (1964); Ollennu (1985); Woodman (1996).

[6] Section 2 of the Ghana Land Law defines an 'allodial title' as the highest or ultimate interest in land held by the State, a stool, skin, family or an individual and may have been acquired through compulsory acquisition, conquest, pioneer discovery and settlement, gift, purchase or agreement.

[7] A 'stool land' is defined by sect 280 of the Ghana Land Law as including land or interest in or right over land controlled by a stool, skin or the head of the particular community, for the benefit of the subjects of that stool, skin or members of that community. A stool is defined as 'stool' including a skin, as well as any person or body of persons having control over skin or community land, as a representative of the particular community. Stool lands are found in Southern Ghana.

[8] A skin in Ghanaian customary law is defined in terms of a stool land but exists in Northern Ghana.

[9] Section 280 of the Land Act defines 'clan land' to include land the allodial title to which is held by a clan or a collection of clans for the benefit of the members of that clan or clans in accordance with customary law and includes land in the parts of the country where a clan or collection of clans is headed by a Tendana.

[10] Family land is defined as 'means land', the allodial title, which is held by a family for the benefit of the members of that family in accordance with customary law.

[11] Hereafter referred to as 'community'.

[12] Hereafter referred to as 'family'.

[13] See the cases of *Ohimien v Adjei* (1957) W.A.L.R 275. See also sect 267(1) of the Constitution.

[14] See sect 20 of the GLA.

The second private interest is a customary freehold acquired up to 22 August 1969.[15] The customary freehold is described as an absolute interest in land that arises from a transaction in customary law, including gift, inheritance, or outright purchase from a community or family that is an allodial title holder.[16] The customary freehold is not subject to any proprietary obligations except in respect of the jurisdictional and cultural rights of an allodial holder, which indicates that indigenous burdens and obligations as recognised by the relevant indigenous law pass with the land. The GLA reiterates that it is of perpetual duration, can be inherited, and is alienable without the consent of the holders of the allodial title. The third private interest is the usufructuary interest that is acquired by a member of the community or family[17] through an express grant by the community or family or by the development of an unappropriated part of community or family land. Usufructuary land can be alienated to a non-indigene with the consent of the appropriate indigenous authority.[18] The fourth interest is customary leasehold acquired that arises if the holder of a community or family allodial title or the holder of a customary freehold or of an usufructuary rights conveys a portion of the land for a specified term and conditions.[19] A customary leasehold may be sublet or assigned. There is no recognition of any burden of customary law. The fifth interest that can be privately held in Ghanaian indigenous land tenure is the customary tenancy that arises where an interest in land is created by contract between the holders of a community or family allodial title or a person who holds a customary law freehold or usufructuary interest for the grant of an interest in land upon agreed terms and conditions.[20] The burden of a customary tenancy may involve the payment of rent, the sharing of the produce of a farm or the physical partition, or severance of the farm or land that arises in two ways for a member of a family or community stool, skin, or family. The first is by an express grant. The second method is a grant of unappropriated land that is subsequently developed.[21]

The GLA reaffirms that the bundle of rights and obligations that attach to indigenous land tenure is in accordance with customary law. The scope of these rights and obligations will vary with the indigenous laws of the community, and such burdens and obligations that are likely to be affirmed by Ghanaian courts. With respect to customary freehold, the jurisdiction, and cultural rights of allodial titles are unclear. Presumably, these rights and obligations would include incidents of respect and customary easements. It is obvious that indigenous law has been amended by the GLA. For example, a customary freehold is an absolute title, and

[15] See sect 3(2) of the GLA.

[16] See sect 3 of the GLA.

[17] See sect 5 of the GLA. An usufructuary interest can also be obtained by a non-indigene who settles on the land for a period of not less than 50 years with the permission of the skin, stool, family, or clan. See sect 5(1)(b) of the GLA.

[18] See sect 5 of the GLA.

[19] See sect 6 of the GLA.

[20] See sect 7 of the GLA.

[21] See sect 5(1)(a) of the Ghana Land Law.

the holder can successfully resist any interference by allodial title holders. The reaffirmation that customary tenure is subject to the customs, traditions, and practices of relevant communities is found in Section 11 of the GLA subject to the prohibition of discriminatory practices on grounds of gender, race, colour, religion, creed, ethnic origin, or social economic status in contravention of Article 17 of the Constitution,[22] certain conclusions are evident from the scheme of the GLA. First, customary law management is separate from common law management and is under the control of a stool, skin, clan, family, and groups according to Article 36 of the Constitution.[23] Second, a significant part of indigenous tenure in Ghana is potentially capable of being privatised, especially when allodial title holders sell communal land to create customary freeholds. Third, the legislative affirmation of gender access based on Ghana's constitutional standards and the jurisprudence of Article 17 which has achieved modest success.

Other African states like Ghana affirm the power of traditional authorities over land and provide a management structure for customary land under their direction, but with broad-based participation of members of a community. First, the GLA provides for questionable mechanisms of accountability such as constituting traditional rulers as fiduciaries in the exercise of management powers vested in them.[24] In Ghana, the management of indigenous land tenure is entrusted to traditional authorities who are regarded as fiduciaries[25] with a duty to be transparent, open, fair, and impartial in their management of the land.[26] The designation of traditional authorities as fiduciaries by the Ghana Land Law is an affirmation of an earlier legislation titled the Head of Family (Accountability) Law of 1985,[27] which is made applicable to the GLA.[28] This law imposes an obligation on any head of family or anyone in control of family property to be accountable for such property to the family, as well as keep records of such property.[29] Kludze points out that the Head of Accountability Law is a reaction to rules of judicial customary law, which had advanced that the Head of the Family is not liable to account for family property.[30] He pointed out that 'living' customary law recognised that the Head of the Family

[22] Article 17 (1) and (2) of the Ghanaian Constitution provides that (1) '(1) All persons shall be equal before the law. (2) A person shall not be discriminated against on grounds of gender, race, colour, ethnic origin, religion, creed or social or economic status.

[23] Article 36(8) of the Ghanaian Constitution. provides that "The State shall recognise that ownership and possession of land carry a social obligation to serve the larger community and, in particular, the State shall recognise that the managers of public, stool, skin and family lands are fiduciaries charged with the obligation to discharge their functions for the benefit respectively of the people of Ghana, of the stool, skin, or family concerned and are accountable as fiduciaries in this regard."

[24] See sect 13(2) of the GLA.

[25] See sect 13(1) of the Ghana Land Act.

[26] Section 13(2) of the Ghana Land Act.

[27] PNDC Law 114.

[28] See sect 13(5) of the CLA.

[29] See sec 1.

[30] See Kludze (1987), pp. 107–118.

has always been held accountable and suggested that the Head of Accountability Law is 'merely declaratory of existing customary law which the courts had been reluctant to enforce'.[31] Furthermore, communities and families holding land are obliged to establish Customary Land Secretariats[32] whose functions in respect of customary interests, rights, and transactions, include the following: (a) record the interests and rights in land, and keep and maintain accurate and up-to-date records of land transactions in the area of operation of the Customary Land Secretariat; (b) provide a list of existing customary interests and rights in land in the area of operation of the Customary Land Secretariat including indication of persons with the capacity to make grants of the interests and rights in that area; (c) provide relevant (i) records on land, (ii) information on hierarchy of interests and rights in land, and (ii) lay down processes for effective dispute resolution; (d) facilitate the settlement of land disputes through alternative dispute resolution; (e) facilitate the participatory preparation of local plans; (f) undertake community education, sensitisation, and awareness creation on land issues; (g) prepare periodic accounts of all revenue received at the Customary Land Secretariats in accordance with clause (8) of Article 36 of the Constitution; (h) provide facilities for search to be conducted on the records on land; and (i) perform any other functions in relation to land as determined by the land-owning group. Available evidence suggests that the existence of 33 customary land secretariats in Ghana[33] of varying degrees of operational efficiency. For example, Akwensivie and Abedi-Lartey recently (2021) identified the Odoitso Odoi Kwao Customary Land Secretariat as the busiest land secretariat in the Greater Accra Region operated by the Odoitso Odoi Kwao family of Accra, and they further state that:

> The 25-member Land Management Committee had successfully resolved 54 land related disputes using Alternative Dispute Resolution mechanisms particularly mediation and customary arbitration. 17 disputes were at various stages of resolution at the time of the appraisal and report writing. The secretariat was well branded. The 36 full-time members of staff included lawyers, licensed surveyors, valuers and estate surveyors. The coordinator of the secretariat also served as the secretary to the family. A total of 2,666 data sets on individual customary land grants had been collected, collated and plotted electronically and plotted manually. It had a fleet of vehicles which were well branded.[34]

Another secretariat is the Gbawe Customary Land Secretariat (Gbawe-Accra) in the Greater Accra Region maintained by the Nii Kortey-Kwatey family. According to Akwensivie and Abedi-Lartey, the record keeping was moderately good. The secretariat kept a log of visitors and staff attendance of between 70 and 85 visitors a week. The 9-member Land Management Committee had successfully resolved more than 70 land disputes with 34 at various stages of resolution through customary arbitration and mediation. The secretariat generated 788 sets of records on customary land grants within its jurisdiction by September 2021. The secretariat also

---

[31] Ibid. 108.

[32] See sect 14(1) of the GLA.

[33] See for example, Akwensivie and Abedi-Lartey (2021), pp. 553–570.

[34] Akwensivie and Abedi-Lartey (2021), p. 554.

kept copies of the indentures on customary land grants made within the jurisdiction.[35]

The authors also reported on two poorly performing Customary Land Secretariats including the Bolga Customary Land Secretariat (Bolga) in the Upper East Region. According to the authors, while the secretariat was actively manned by five persons, including an administrator, the 23-member Land Management Committee was not active due to several reasons, including marked disagreements among the various Tindaamas resulting in a dormant Tindaama association; marked disagreements between the Tindaama and the chiefs, which negatively affected the operations of the secretariat.[36] The authors assessed that: 'Not more than 14 land-related disputes had been resolved by the Land Management Committee. 211 customary land grants had been recorded since 2008 and these had been disaggregated by gender'.[37] The Customary Land Secretariates and the Bongo Customary Land Secretariat in the Upper East Region declare that the secretariat and the Land Management Committee were not active at the time of the appraisal.[38] The authors generally consider the Customary Land Secretariats as failing in their duty to maintain accurate and up-to-date records of land transactions, but successful in using alternative dispute resolution mechanisms.[39] They recommend institutional human resources and technological improvements, strongly suggesting that, in general, Customary Land Secretariats have assisted in managing the privatisation of indigenous land in Ghana.

In sum, there is therefore little doubt that indigenous law is contemplated in the process of the privatisation of indigenous land tenure.

2.2 Kenya

Kenya is an East African country made up of the following ethnic groups: Kikuyu 17.1%, Luhya 14.3%, Kalenjin 13.4%, Luo 10.7%, Kamba 9.8%, Somali 5.8%, Kisii 5.7%, Mijikenda 5.2%, Meru 4.2%, Maasai 2.5%, Turkana 2.1%, non-Kenyan 1%, and others at 8.2%. The country's urban population is estimated at 29.5% of the total population in 2023.[40]

---

[35] Ibid. 556.

[36] Ibid. 568

[37] Ibid.

[38] Akwensivie and Abedi-Lartey (2021), p. 568.

[39] Ibid 569.

[40] Kenya's administrative divisions are 47 countries: Baringo, Bomet, Bungoma, Busia, Elgeyo/Marakwet, Embu, Garissa, Homa Bay, Isiolo, Kajiado, Kakamega, Kericho, Kiambu, Kilifi, Kirinyaga, Kisii, Kisumu, Kitui, Kwale, Laikipia, Lamu, Machakos, Makueni, Mandera, Marsabit, Meru, Migori, Mombasa, Murang'a, Nairobi City, Nakuru, Nandi, Narok, Nyamira, Nyandarua, Nyeri, Samburu, Siaya, Taita/Taveta, Tana River, Tharaka-Nithi, Trans Nzoia, Turkana, Uasin Gishu, Vihiga, Wajir, and West Pokot.

Community land is recognised by Section 61 of the 2010 Kenyan Constitution as equal to public and private land. Community land in Kenya is vested and held by communities identified based on ethnicity, culture, or similar community of interest.[41] Community land is defined as including:

> (a) land lawfully registered in the name of group representatives under the provisions of any law; (b) land lawfully transferred to a specific community by any process of law; (c) any other land declared to be community land by an Act of Parliament; and (d) land that is— (i) lawfully held, managed or used by specific communities as community forests, grazing areas or shrines; (ii) ancestral lands and lands traditionally occupied by hunter-gatherer communities; or (iii) lawfully held as trust land by the county governments, but not including any public land held in trust by the county government.[42]

Other constitutional provisions on community land include the prohibition of the disposal of such land except in terms of legislation specifying the nature and extent of the rights of members of each community individually and collectively.[43] The Community Land Act 2016[44] was enacted in furtherance of a constitutional direction to parliament to enact legislation to give effect to Article 63 of the Constitution.[45]

The vesting of radical title in communities is found in the Community according to the Kenyan Community Land Act of 2016. Section 4 of the Community Land Act of 2016 declares that community land shall vest in the community and also that the Kenyan state may regulate the use of community land in accordance with Article 66 of the 2010 Constitution.[46] Community land is declared to include customary freehold and leasehold tenures[47] and may be held as communal land, family or clan land, or reserve land. It appears obvious that the idea of community land is primarily informed by customary land tenure, although there is a clear intention that community land is wider than customary land. Since customary land rights are defined as referring to rights conferred or derived from customs and practices consistent with African customary law,[48] it is important to bear in mind that customary land is part of community land, but different and distinct. What the CLA does is to affirm the status of customary land and its equal status to other land tenures, such as freehold and leasehold. This is evident in three provisions of the CLA. First, Section 5(5) validates subsisting customary law rights at the time of the commencement of the

---

[41] See sect 63(1) of the Kenyan Constitution.

[42] Section 63(2).

[43] Section 63(4).

[44] No. 27 of 2016.

[45] Section 63(5). See also the Community Land Regulations 2017.

[46] Article 66 (1) of the Kenyan Constitution provides that. (1) The State may regulate the use of any land, or any interest in or right over any land, in the interest of defence, public safety, public order, public morality, public health, or land use planning.

[47] Section 4(3) of the Community Land Act 2016.

[48] See sect 2 of the Community Land Act.

Act[49] and Section 5(3) provides that customary land rights shall be 'recognised, adjudicated for and documented for purposes of registration …'. A third provision is Section 14(3), which recognises existing derivative customary rights of occupancy. The registration of a customary community as the proprietor of land or lease shall vest in that community absolute ownership of that land.[50] Accordingly, an elaborate procedure for registration is contained in paragraphs 8–11 of the CLA Regulations 2017. The Community Land Management Committee shall apply to the Registrar for the registration of the community. The application shall be accompanied by the name of the community; a register of members of the community; a certified true copy of the minutes of the meeting at which it was resolved to seek an application for registration; rules and regulations of the community; a description of the interest in land being claimed by the community, including a sketch map. Upon registration, the community named in the certificate of registration shall be a body corporate, in the name specified in the certificate, with perpetual succession and a common seal; and shall in its corporate name, subject to the Act and the conditions, limitations, and exemptions in the certificate of registration, be capable of suing and being sued; acquiring, holding, charging, or disposing of movable or immovable property; and having and managing its own funds including borrowing and lending money; and doing or performing such other things or acts necessary for the proper performance of its functions which may lawfully be done by a body corporate.

The members of the Community Land Management Committee become the officers of the community; be responsible for management of any property of the community; exercise their powers on behalf and for the collective benefit of all members of the community; and consult the community assembly on such exercise of their powers. It is clear that the provisions of the CLA do not create customary land since these lands are antecedent to the CLA and indeed the Kenyan state. What the Kenyan CLA has been hailed[51] as achieving is the clear legislative and constitutional intent of elevating indigenous tenure from an inferior title to a superior title equal to a freehold.[52] In fact, Section 16 of the CLA provides that the registration of a community as a proprietor vests in the community '… the absolute ownership of the land together with all the rights and privileges of such ownership'.

Individual members of an indigenous community can have customary rights of occupancy, as well as customary tenancies as derivative rights of the community in terms of Sections 14 and 27(1)[53] and (2)[54] of the CLA. The customary rights of occupancy envisaged by Section 14 are of indefinite duration, governed by

[49] The CLA commenced on September 21 2016.

[50] See sect 16 of the CLA.

[51] See Oloo et al. (2021) and Alden Wiley (2018).

[52] See also Di Matteo (2021).

[53] Section 27(1) of the CLA states that customary rights of occupancy shall not be issued as a separate title from customary land.

[54] Section 27(2) reaffirms that customary rights of occupancy shall not be superior to the title of the customary community.

customary law in respect of any dealings, and equal in status to other rights of occupancy.[55] Paragraph 16 of the Community Land Regulations requires the assent of at least two-thirds of the community assembly to sell community land or allocate community land to its members. The transfer instrument shall, upon approval, be presented for registration in terms of the Land Registration Act of 2012. The same procedure presumably applies to the allocation of community land to community members. Section 18 of the CLA regards the certificate of title issued to a purchaser of community land as *prima facie* evidence that the person who is named in the title is the absolute and indefeasible owner of the land subject to encumbrances, easements, restrictions, and conditions contained or endorsed in the certificate. The extent of the rights granted by the Committee shall be contained in a survey and map that should be forwarded to the Registrar of Land to be noted in the Community Land Register in accordance with the Land Registration Act of 2012. Paragraph 16 of the Community Land Regulations 2017 recognise the conversion of community land to private land, suggesting the contemplation of an organised process for the privatisation of communal indigenous land tenure. A community may convert the whole or part of its land to private land through a transfer with the approval of at least two-thirds of the community assembly. Upon approval under paragraph 16 of the CLR, a transfer instrument is prepared and executed by the Chairman and Secretary of the Community Land Management Committee and presented to the Registrar for registration in accordance with the Land Registration Act. After approval, a community may allocate a whole or part of its land to the members in accordance with the Act, with the approval of at least two-thirds of the community assembly.

The sale or allocation of community rights of occupancy is subject to community trusts. The principle of customary trusts in Kenya arose from an interpretation of the Kenyan Registered Land Act that registration of a customary tenure extinguished customary interests. In *Kiebia v M'lintari,*[56] the Supreme Court described the concept of a customary trust as including registered land that prior to registration,

> … always reserved for family or clan uses, such as burials, and other traditional rites. It could also be that other parts of the land, depending on the specific group or family setting, were reserved for various future uses, such as construction of houses and other amenities by youths graduating into manhood.

The legislative framework around which the concept of registered land was recognised included Section 28(a) of the repealed Registered Land Act which provided that 'the registration of a person as the proprietor of land shall vest in that person the absolute ownership of that land together with all rights and privileges belonging or appurtenant thereto'. A line of cases interpreting this provision, including *Esiroyo v*

---

[55] See sect 5 of the Kenyan Land Act 2012 that provides for freehold leasehold and other forms of partial interest in land.

[56] [2018] eKLR.

Esiroyo[57] and *Obiero v Obiero*[58] had held that registration extinguished all rights, including customary rights. Section 25 of the 2012 Land Registration Act provides for the extinguishment of rights, but with a caveat that qualifies the extinguishment of rights to the extent that obligations of the proprietor as a trustee are preserved. These would include customary trusts for which the Supreme Court in *Kiebia vM'lintari* set out the requirements, including that the land in question was before registration, family, clan or group land. Second, the claimant belongs to such a family, clan, or group, and third, the relationship of the claimant to such a family, clan, or group is not so remote or tenuous as to make their claim idle or adventurous. Fourth, the claimant could have been entitled to be registered as an owner or other beneficiary of the land but for some intervening circumstances. Lastly, the claim is directed against the registered proprietor who is a member of the family, clan, or group. Sections 17 and 18 of the CLA recognise customary trusts.

Section 27 of the CLA envisages a customary tenancy that is a right to exclusive use and occupancy of land for a definite period granted to an individual and is not superior to community title in any way. The incidents of a customary tenancy include payment of a fee for use to a registered community; development in accordance with land use laws; non-assignment or lease to non-members of a community; lawful use; and surrender to the registered community when quiet enjoyment is no longer feasible.[59]

In addition to customary tenancies, other special rights and entitlements envisaged on community land include grazing rights. The CLA emphasises the access and use by members of pastoral communities of communal land for livestock grazing, subject to conditions including the kind and number of livestock as well as the grazing area.[60] Non-members of the community may be granted grazing rights by the community.[61]

In granting customary rights of occupancy and customary tenancies, the community must consider the equal treatment of applications by men and women, as well as the need to ensure non-discrimination based on gender, disability, minority culture, or marital status.[62] Kenya's Constitution[63] and judiciary[64] provide for, and enforce, gender equality.

It is fair to argue that the privatisation of indigenous land tenure in Kenya is significantly within the framework of indigenous law because the customary rights of occupancy are derived from the registered community. In addition to community

[57] 1973 EA 338.

[58] 1972 EA 277.

[59] See sect 27(4) of the CLA.

[60] See sect 28(2) of the CLA.

[61] See sect 28(3) of the CLA.

[62] See sects 14(4) and 30 of the CLA.

[63] Article 27 of the Kenyan Constitution calls for equality between men and women in decision-making, access, and participation.

[64] See the case of *Cheruiyot v Korir* [2017] eKLR.

trusts, customary communities appear to have the capacity to impose conditions, encumbrances, and easements on customary rights of occupancy allocated or sold to members and non-members of the community. In other words, the nature and extent of customary rights of occupancy depend on the capacity of the Land Management Committee of the registered community to manage community land.

In Kenya, the management of community land is entrusted to the Community Land Management Committees. The Committee is envisioned to be constituted of between seven and fifteen members of the Community Assembly, which is made up of adult members of the community, with a quorum of two-thirds of the members.[65] The membership of the Committee must reflect geographical considerations, cultural diversity, the two-thirds gender rule, special interests, youth, and persons with disabilities in the community. The functions of these management structures suggest the depth of their influence. For example, the functioning of the Kenyan Community Land Management Committee[66] include running the day-to-day tasks of the Committee; managing and administering the registered community land; coordinating the development of community land-use plans; promoting the participation of community members in the management of registered community land, and prescribing rules and regulations to govern operations of the community. While the Committee may approve decisions by a simple majority of community members, it is only in respect of the alienation of community land that approval of at least two-thirds majority of the registered community members is needed. These functions indicate that the outcomes of the privatisation of indigenous tenure are heavily dependent on the quality of the membership of the Land Management Committee and the discharge of their functions. The function of prescribing rules for the operation of community land is crucial to the manner in which privatisation is to be carried out. For example, the second schedule to the Community Land Act Regulations 2017 sets out issues that Community Land Management Rules should and gives an idea of how the development of these rules could affect the management of the community and, in turn, affect the privatisation of indigenous land tenure. For example, the Rules should reflect: 'A description and extent of the land which the community has, under recognized customary law, exercised rights of use and occupation'. The Third Schedule contains Model Rules to guide the development of Community Land Management Rules that also indicate how the privatisation of indigenous land tenure may be managed and includes membership rules of a registered community. Paragraph 4 of the Model Rules define a member to include: '(a) Members whose names are in the register of members of the community upon registration; (ii) new persons born and married in the community; (ii) a person who has inherited an interest from a person whose name is in the register of members; (iii) a person the community land management committee members all agree should be a member; and the community land management committee member's decision is confirmed at a community assembly; and (iv) a court so orders'. Persons who

[65] See sect 15(3) of the CLA.

[66] See sect 15(4) of the CLA.

purchase community land are potentially members of a community if the Community Land Management Committee indicates membership as a condition for the alienation of community land. In that case, such persons may be nominated and approved to be members of the community. The rights of members are also set out in the Third Schedule and govern how community land may be alienated, and the consequences of alienation. These rights include the right to share in the ownership of the community land in undivided shares; reside free of charge on the community land together with their family and dependants; use of land and water rights in the community subject to such conditions as may from time to time be imposed in accordance with these rules and regulations, which may include the levy of access, fees or other charges; to attend, speak and be heard, and to vote at all community assemblies of the community; disposition of any of the community land, or any interest therein, may be made except with the approval of two-thirds adult members in a community assembly. There are obligations on members that include observing and complying with all the community's rules and regulations and decisions taken by the Community Land Management Committee if ratified by the Community Assembly; meeting the debts of the community in accordance with the provisions of the Act and these rules and by-laws; paying fees or other charges; contributing such labour as may be reasonably required. Academic commentary on the management of community land is mixed. Although there is criticism of the nature of the title of the community, as well as the processes and entitlements that the different institutions that manage community land receive, there is more concern with the registration of communities that endow radical title to the community land[67] and other issues, such as women's participation in the management of the community land.[68]

It is easy to conclude from the available evidence that the privatisation of indigenous land in the indigenous communities of Kenya is intricately tied to communal ownership and management, and this bodes well for the future of indigenous law.

2.3 *Uganda*

An estimate of Uganda's population in 2024 is roughly 50 million people with the following major ethnic groups: Baganda; Banyankole; Basoga; Bakiga; Iteso; Langi; Bagisu; Acholi; Lugbara; and others, with an urban population of about 27%.[69]

In Uganda, Article 237(3) of the 1995 Constitution recognises customary land tenure as one of the four main land tenure systems in the country through which Ugandans can own land. Interestingly, the Constitution declares that land in Uganda

[67] See Odote, Rahma and others (2021), p. 291.

[68] Ibid 303: 'The passing of the Community Land Act was a landmark development in Kenya after several false starts and a long delay. The hope that it would translate to improved recognition and protection of community land in the country has been hampered by slow and half-hearted implementation of the law.'

[69] See https://www.cia.gov/the-world-factbook/countries/uganda/.

belongs to the citizens of Uganda[70] but provides for customary land tenure that is inherently communal. Two other provisions concerning customary land tenure in Uganda are important. Citizens who own land under customary tenure are eligible to acquire certificates of ownership and can convert such land to freehold land ownership. The Land Act of 1998 was enacted to elaborate on the constitutional protection of customary land tenure.

The 1998 Ugandan Land Act recognises customary freehold Mailo and leasehold land tenures. A customary tenure applies to specific areas of land governed by rules generally accepted as binding by members of the customary community and using local customary management rules.[71] In *River Oli Local Government v Okoya*,[72] a Ugandan High Court held that ownership of customary tenure of a specific area of Uganda can be proved in three ways. The first is through the provisions of codified customary law[73] and the second is through the judicial notice of customary practices;[74] and third, through proof of facts.

Customary tenure envisages communal and individual ownership and use of land.[75] Private interest in communal and family customary tenure is through a usufructuary right that,

> A usufructuary enjoys exclusive rights over land allotted to her, but subject to the overriding interests of the family. For the duration of the usufruct the rest of the members of the family could not interfere with her peaceful possession and use of the land subject to usufruct, for as long as that use was consistent with the group nature of the ownership and the enjoyment of the land by future generations.[76]

Private ownership of customary tenure can be represented by a certificate of customary ownership that a Parish Committee can issue.[77] The Ugandan Supreme Court in *Okello v Attorney General* recognises that individual ownership must meet the demands of socio-economic development in Uganda.[78] Clearly, the sale of a customary tenancy is inchoate without a certificate of customary ownership. Consequently, the Parish Committee determines rights boundaries, rights of way,

---

[70] Article 237 of the Ugandan Constitution.

[71] See sect 3 of the Ugandan Land Act 1998 (hereafter ULA). See *River Oli Division Local Government v Okoya* [2016] UGHCCD 62.

[72] Ibid.

[73] Examples of codified customary law include legislation such as the Ankole Landlord and Tenant Law 1937.

[74] Section 56(3) of the Uganda Evidence Act empowers courts to take judicial notice of facts.

[75] Ibid.

[76] See *Auma v Kidega & Another* [2020] UGHC 117.

[77] Ibid sects 4, 5 and 6.

[78] Paragraphs 39–40. Note para 40: 'As a result, over time, there has been evolution of tenure in Uganda and land has been undergoing individualization and change through post-independence legislations; Public Lands Act 1962 and 1969, Land Reform Decree 1975, the 1995 Constitution of Uganda and the Land Act 1998'.

and easements in accordance with applicable customary law and makes recommendations to the Parish Committee, and issues a certificate of customary ownership subject to express conditions of land tenure. A certificate of customary ownership is conclusive evidence of the customary rights and incidents contained in it.[79] Accordingly, the holder of the certificate can lease, grant an usufructuary right, mortgage or pledge the land, subdivide or assign the land, sell the land, dispose of the land by testamentary instruments, subject to the recording of the transaction. A registered certificate of customary ownership confers rights similar to rights of a freehold tenure. Furthermore, a holder of a customary tenure may apply to convert the tenure to a freehold tenure which confers absolute ownership of the land on the holder. Conversion changes the form of ownership from the previous customary ownership to the expected or desired freehold ownership by registration.[80]

The definition and incidents of customary tenure strongly suggest a tenuous hold of indigenous law on customary tenure in Uganda as envisaged by the ULA. While the expressly indicated incidents of customary tenure follow the incidents of a freehold tenure, there is only a general acknowledgement that customary tenure is subject to indigenous law. Furthermore, control over customary tenure incidents lies with the Parish Committee and the Land Boards, further eroding the idea of any meaningful control of customary tenure by indigenous authorities. Rather, the ULA has elevated the Parish Committee and the Land Boards above indigenous authorities. Consequently, it can be concluded that the ULA has privatised communal land tenure outside the framework of indigenous law. The exact parameters of this framework are not very clear.

The fact that customary land can be converted to a freehold property and not vice versa surely indicates that such conversion is intended to endow Ugandans with the freedom that comes with freehold property. Whether such a conversion extinguishes the incidents of customary tenure is a live point, although it is likely. The Ugandan Supreme Court in Okello did not address this point, and it is likely that, given the definition of a freehold property, the conversion extinguishes incidents of customary law.

Uganda's privatisation of indigenous land tenure has been supported by the Mortgage Act 2009 (8 of 2009) which recognises the creation and operation of mortgages on individual customary land based on customary law[81] which was the contention point in several cases, including *Uganda Ecumenical Church Loan Fund Ltd v Nankabirwa Harriet.*[82]

The Ugandan Supreme Court reviewed the status of individual customary tenure in *Okello v Attorney General* in a terse paragraph:

> This takes me to the last aspect about the marginalisation of land held under customary tenure. I do not agree with the petitioners that the law marginalises any Land tenure system.

---

[79] Ibid sect 8.

[80] See *Bunyoro Kitara Reparation Agency Ltd v Masindi District Land Board* [2022] UGCLD 100.

[81] Section 9.

[82] [2006] UGCommC 50.

> What the [aw does is to define what customary Land tenure is, the incidents thereof as set out under section 3 of the Land Act, for instance, the law provides that it is Land held in perpetuity. Other characteristics of what customary tenure system entails is that, it is governed by or regulated by the customs and practices of the community where the land is situate. Even when land under customary tenure is bought, it remains regulated by the customs and practices applicable to it unless or until it is converted to freehold tenure. Further the land can be acquired in a manner accepted under the customary [laws, norms or practices of a particular community. The applicable customs to the Land would determine whether the land would be risky for purposes of being used as a security for a mortgage or for a loan. For instance, if the individual ownership cannot be pledged or sold without clan permission, (hypothetically at least), a financial institution might prefer freehold title which is held at the pleasure of the individual who may sell or dispose of the Land without consulting anybody except as set out in the Land Act.[83]

In holding that the Ugandan vision of customary land tenure is valid but inadequately enforced, the Okello Court missed an opportunity to strengthen the customary land tenure system at the behest of the Aholi tribe that sought greater involvement of their customary law structures in the work of Area and District Committees through mandatory consultations in the allocation, conversion, and registration of customary tenure. The Court recognised this point by stating that: 'Petitioners only seek to have a greater role for customary institutions in applications for certificates of customary ownership or to convert customary owned Land to freehold tenure, which is a matter best left for Parliament to determine'.[84]

When African judiciaries shrink from a judicial responsibility to strengthen customary law systems, the system's plight is exacerbated, making it more difficult to manage the privatisation of indigenous land tenure to the latter's benefit. The greater involvement of customary institutions in registration would improve the recognition of the multiple and interlocking secondary rights that are often a feature of customary tenure. Involving these institutions in the conversion of freehold could assist in the development of formal and informal obligations by the freehold owner in the survival of the indigenous land tenure. To turn to statutory reform as suggested by the lead judgment of Madarama JCC and Mugenyi JCC in *Okello v Attorney General*, as a substitute for the Court mandating a greater involvement of customary authorities was a missed opportunity to address the inadequate enforcement of the customary land tenure systems, rather than stress the point that inadequate enforcement of the customary land tenure is not a constitutional matter.

The importance of the involvement of customary authorities in the management of customary land in general and the conversion of customary tenancy to freehold is demonstrated by the case of *Jagwe v Bugingo*,[85] where the parties struggled to establish whether there was a customary tenancy of a piece of land that a Lands Board had registered. However the Court of Appeal held that an Area Land Committee 'has the power to determine who qualifies as a customary owner'[86] a

[83] Paragraph 92.

[84] At p 104.

[85] [2022] UGCA 107.

[86] At p 11.

function that can be facilitated by the involvement of customary authorities. Furthermore, the Court of Appeal held that there was no customary tenancy when, in fact, the customary functionaries may have demonstrated that such a tenancy exists.[87] The privatisation of indigenous tenure appears to unleash an impulse to alienate communal and family land. The ULA specifically requires the consent of the family to alienate family land because it provides in Section 39 that a member of the family shall sell, exchange, transfer, pledge, mortgage, or lease family land.[88]

In conclusion, the conversion of customary land into freehold land poses a considerable risk to the survival of communal indigenous tenure. It appears evident that individual customary land tenure is free from the usual strictures of indigenous land tenure. However, the spatial location of an individual customary law within family or communal land is likely to lead to certain customary obligations in addition to conditions that may be attached to the sale or lease of customary land.

2.4 South Africa

European contact with South Africa's indigenous communities from the seventeenth century to the early decades of the twentieth century is a history of gradual encroachment on their land tenure but a significant portion of this land tenure was communal.[89] According to Du Plessis and Pienaar, 'During the period 1913 to 1991, several pieces of legislation were introduced to regulate communal land tenure in accordance with a government policy of segregation'. As the size and strength of the communal land tenure decreased, the occupational and possessory rights for South Africans increased. By the time South Africa became a constitutional democracy in 1993, which also constitutionally recognised customary law, one of the fundamental challenges of South Africa's tenurial relations was how to ensure a more democratic and accountable indigenous land tenure management, generally,[90] including how to ensure that individual tenure ownership thrives within or outside a communal land tenure framework. South Africa's Apartheid government and colonial rule[91] recognised communal land tenure in several parts of South Africa and user rights for South Africans, mostly outside the areas where communal land tenure was established through a combination of legislation. They included the Black Land Act 27 of 1913; the Black Administration Act 38 of 1927; the Development Trust and Land Act 18 of 1936; and the Black Authorities Act of 1951. Although individual land

[87] See Dieterle (n.d.), pp. 582–589.

[88] See *Wamamo v Equity Bank*; *Ntare v Equity Bank* [2015] UGCommC 20.

[89] See for example Wilson et al. (2000).

[90] For an overview mostly critical of the Apartheid legacy of communal land tenure, see the following: Du Plessis and Pienaar (2010), pp. 73–89. See also Van der Walt (1995), pp. 1–30; Feinberg (2009), pp. 39–61.

[91] See para 10 of *Togaoane v Minister of Agriculture and Land Affairs* [2010] ZACC 10 for a summary of these policies and discriminatory land practices.

tenure existed outside communal land tenure areas such as in the Bantustans[92] as stated above, the possibility of individual land holding in South Africa's communal land tenure areas was firmly laid by the occupational and possessory rights available to non-white South Africans, such that the privatisation of individual tenure before the dawn of constitutional rule in 1993 was at the discretion of indigenous communities. Decades of racial application of tenure legislation by the Apartheid government led to the large displacement of millions of black South Africans, such that the restitution of communal and individual land to persons who were disposed of such lands after 1913 was a focus of the 1996 Constitution that mandated legislation to address these past injustices[93] including insecure tenure.

The constitutional tenure of land reform is found in Section 25 of the Constitution, which provides for the redistribution of land by Section 25(5), for the restitution of land by Section 25(7),[94] and tenure reform by Section 25(6). Although the complex and interlocking perspectives of communal land tenure in South Africa involved these three perspectives, the issue of privatisation of communal land tenure is most relevant in tenure reform. The constitutional imperative for land reform is articulated in the White Paper on South African Land Policy and includes an overarching protection of insecure rights, existing at the time of the advent of constitutional democracy aptly described as insecure rights; and second, extensive and fundamental tenure reform that would recognise exclusive individual land holding within communal land tenure as well as more accountable and democratic communal land tenure management frameworks. The benefit of hindsight reveals that this two-pronged approach ensured that since the protection of insecure land rights was immediate, the failure of extensive land tenure reform would ensure that decades after the failed attempt to extensively reform communal land tenure through the Communal Land Rights Act 2004, it is the protection of insecure rights that remains the framework of land reform of communal land tenure. While the protection of insecure tenure rights often transformed the insecure occupational and possessory rights of non-white South Africans into secure individual land-holding, communal and family land-holding also benefited from the strengthening of insecure rights.

The protection of existing insecure land rights proceeded through two legislations which are the Interim Protection of Informal Land Rights Act (IPILRA) of 1996 and the Upgrading of Land Tenure Act (ULTRA) of 1991 as amended. ULTRA 1991 had begun in the Apartheid era and was designed to automatically upgrade existing land tenure or upgrade such tenure in accordance with laid-down

---

[92] The 'Bantustans' refer to independent homelands created by the Apartheid government, such as Transkei and Ciskei.

[93] See sect 25(6) of the 1996 Constitution which provides that: 'A person or community whose tenure of land is legally insecure as a result of past racially discriminatory laws or practices is entitled, to the extent provided by an Act of Parliament, either to tenure which is legally secure or to comparable redress.'

[94] Section 25(7) provides: 'A person or community dispossessed of property after 19 June 1913 as a result of past racially discriminatory laws or practices is entitled, to the extent provided by an Act of Parliament, either to restitution of that property or to equitable redress.'

procedures. The reach of ULTRA 1991 and numerous amendments in upgrading individual land rights in communal land tenure is questionable, since customary law and traditional authorities that underpin communal land tenure and individual land use are constitutionally recognised. However, the IPLIRA 1996 was designed to ensure that *de facto* individual rights, including some that were in communal land tenure areas, could only be extinguished after due process that includes compliance with the custom and usage of that community[95] expressed through a vote of the majority of members of a community,[96] and payment of appropriate compensation.[97] Neither Acts enable the privatisation of communal land without the consent of traditional authorities, but indirectly protect some individual land interests that existed at the advent of South Africa's constitutional democracy in 1996. For example, judicial interpretation has recognised holders of informal rights in land, including families holding forms of communal land tenure who are entitled to be consulted in terms of providing consent to the expropriation of land, evident in the cases of *Maledu and Others v Itereleng Bakgatla Mineral Resources (Pty) Ltd;*[98] *Baleni and Others v Minister of Mineral Resources and Others;*[99] and *Alexkhor v Richtersveld Community.*[100] As stated above, these tenurial improvement legislations did not extend to communally held land,[101] and whether this deficiency is material in South Africa is debatable, given that only about 13% of South Africa's land mass is communal land tenure, with individual land holdings in and around communal land tenure areas that would have been greater if not for centuries of European contact colonisation and appropriation.

As stated above, restitution of land is another concept of land tenure reform of communal land tenure that indirectly affects the possibility of privatising communal land tenure. The South African Parliament passed the Restitution of Land Rights Act 22 of 1994, which defined a community as 'any group of persons whose rights on land are derived from shared rules determining access to and held in common by such group'.[102] This Act enabled the Communal Property Association Act 28 of 1996, which facilitated the process of restitution of communal land through an option for the establishment of a Communal Property Association (CPA) as a

[95] See sect 2(2) of IPILRA.

[96] See sect 2(4) of IPLIRA.

[97] See sect 2(3) of IPLIRA.

[98] [2018] ZACC 41.

[99] [2018] ZAGPPHC 829.

[100] [2003] ZACC 18.

[101] It must be acknowledged that there is case law where occupational rights, such as Permissions to Occupy (PTO), were effective in excising indigenous land tenure from family and communal control. See for example Herbert N.O. and Others v Senqu Municipality and Others [2021] ZASCA 177.

[102] See the following literature on the operation of the RLRA 1994: Christopher (1995), Hall (2004), Roux (2006)

juristic person to acquire, hold, and manage property, including restituted land.[103] Several communities opt for the use of CPAs that operates within a framework that recognises the capacity of these communities to agree on tenurial relations[104] including how individual land tenure can be recognised[105] perhaps to facilitate and promote the objectives of Section 25(5) of the Constitution of the Republic of South Africa, 1996 (Constitution) that recognises the need for citizens to acquire land on an equitable basis. Along this line, a 2024 amendment to the CPA clarifies that land in a CPA shall include parts of the land for residential industrial and commercial purposes rather than all be ownership by the association thereby securing individual ownership. In addition to CPAs, there is no impediment for indigenous communities to establish a Communal Land Trust, or Section 21 registered in terms of the Companies Act 1973 which may in turn form CPAs.

With the advent of Community Property Associations representing communal land tenure of indigenous communities, the communal tenure that exists in South Africa is first state land, as land allocated by the state to communities;[106] bought land, as land purchased by the community; and claimed lands in terms of land held and managed by Communal Property Associations[107] collectively or through a designated council or persons.

Members of the community have residential business and residential user rights on the payment of annual levies, and such land cannot be sold or alienated, a position affirmed by a South African High Court in *Maloka v Mosimane.*[108] Third parties could elect community members and pay annual levies to acquire user rights. Communal land tenure in South Africa amounts to between 14 and 15% of South Africa and is largely characterised by communal and family land,[109] including the indigenous tenure in KwaZulu-Natal that is governed under the control of the Zulu King by the Ingonyama Trust[110]

Considerable advocacy for reforming the indigenous land tenure system to include individual land tenure led to the introduction of the Communal Land Rights Act (CLRA),[111] which was struck down by the Constitutional Court in *Togoane v*

[103] See for example the case of Mamohola Community Property Association v Molewa [2022] ZALMPHC 10. Note also the provisions of sec 2 of Community Property Association Act.

[104] See the case of Mpheleng Communal Property Association v Kgoshigadi Mathebe of Bantwane Traditional Community [2025] ZALCC 24 and Sangoni v Tshemese [2018] ZAECMHC 53.

[105] See Baphuting Bo Seleka Community v Borakologadi Communal Property Association [2017] ZALCC 7. See also Weinberg (2021).

[106] This is land owned by the state through the National Minister of Rural Development and Land Affairs from time immemorial, but proclaimed for and administered by a specific community.

[107] See Maila, Raboshakga and others (2023), pp. 41–42.

[108] [2013] ZANHWC 8. See Du Plessis and Frantz (2013).

[109] See Delius, Beinart (2021), pp. 84–109.

[110] Established by the Ingonyama Trust Act (No 3KZ of 1994).

[111] 11 of 2004.

Minister of Agriculture and Land Affairs.[112] The CLRA was declared constitutionally invalid for pre-enactment irregularity of improper tagging. However, it is essential to note the provisions of the Act that generated considerable opposition because they give a telling commentary on the possibility of privatising communal land tenure in South Africa, which forms part of the comprehensive land tenure reform alluded to above. In the main, stakeholder discontent with the 2004 Communal Land Rights Act was across the board for different reasons. Traditional authorities were aggrieved with the CLRA for several reasons, including discomfort with formalisation and alignment of individual titles.[113] Other stakeholders argued that the composition of the land administration committees contemplated undemocratic and unaccountable traditional councils,[114] whose patriarchal tendencies[115] are not cured by the somewhat broad-based membership of the Council if it acts as a land administration committee.[116] The overbearing powers of the Minister of Rural Development in respect of the formal processes of the CLRA were also an issue.

A 2017 bill[117] was introduced to cure some of the defects in the CLRA. For example, Clause 9(2)(a) of the Bill contemplates the transfer of ownership of subdivided communal land occupied by a community member to that community member. All subsequent individual land rights in community land must be determined by the Community according to Clause 11 of the Bill which sets out these rights to include ownership; rights to use, lease, or other property rights.[118] Clause 12 deals with registration of communal land and requires that communal land should be registered in the name of the community and subdivided in the name of the community member. Clause 13 restricts alienation of communal land by sale, lease, or other encumbrances without a written resolution of the community. Furthermore,

---

[112] [2010] ZACC 10. See the following commentary on the decision: Mailula (2011); and Mostert (2010).

[113] See Chapter 3 (Transfer and Registration of Communal Land) of the Act.

[114] See chapter 7 of the Act. Note for example sect 21(2): 'If a community has a recognised traditional council, the powers and duties of the land administration committee of such community may be exercised and performed by such council.'

[115] See the following literature of the impact of the Communal Land Rights Act 2004 on rural women: Claassens and Ngubane (Legal 2008), p. 154; Cousins (2013), pp. 73–99.

[116] Section 22 of the CLRA contemplates that if the Traditional Council is not acting as the Land Administration Committee, one-third of the total membership must be women and one member must represent the interests of vulnerable community members, including women, children and the youth, the elderly and the disabled. See the following Dlamini 'Landownership' 42. Also see Kingwill (2017), p. 65; Chenitz and Richardson (2013), p. 113.

[117] See Government Gazette, 7 July 2017 (No 40965).

[118] Clause 11 provides as follows: **11.** (1) A community whose land rights have been converted into ownership or to whom ownership of land has been transferred after the commencement of this Act in terms of section 9 must, by means of its community rules, determine the nature of rights to a subdivided portion of communal land designated for residential, industrial or commercial purposes. (2) The nature of rights contemplated in subsection (1) include— *(a)* ownership in the case of land owned or occupied by or transferred to a community; and *(b)* right to use, lease or any other right relating to property as may exist in law.

members of a family that owns land and of the community and the South African state have a first option to subdivided land.

The Bill also supports the ability of communities whose ownership of communal land is transferred to decide by a resolution of not less than 60% of households from the community whether to choose either a traditional council or a community property association or any other entity to manage or administer communal land on its behalf.[119]

Whether the 2017 Bill improves the CLRA is an open question, as the *status quo* remains that members of communities only have a use right in communal land and, at best, an ownership right at the discretion of the indigenous community in South Africa. Another innovation contemplated by the 2017 Bill is the articulation of community rules which is essentially a development of indigenous law. In this regard, Clause 25 of the Bill declares that a community to which land is transferred becomes a juristic person upon receipt of a Deed of Communal Land whose rules can be adopted by 60% of the households of such a community. These rules must regulate the general management and administration of communal land; the nature of rights to subdivided portions of communal land; the alienation or termination of rights other than ownership rights; the allocation of subdivided portions of communal land; the keeping of a communal land register; the use of communal land by the entire community, households and persons in general; the sale, donation, lease, encumbrance, or any alienation of rights to communal land; the use of communal land by persons or legal entities other than those from the relevant community; and administration fees. The process of making and adopting community rules must be guided by the following principles: fair and inclusive decision-making; equality; access to communal property; accountability and transparency; and democratic processes governing the conduct of community meetings.

In conclusion, indigenous land tenure continues to exist in South Africa and the possibility of privatisation is at the discretion of indigenous communities.

2.5 Liberia

Liberia passed the Land Rights Act (LRA) in 2018[120] to deal with customary land that occupies approximately 70% of Liberia's land mass. The purpose of the LRA is Customary Land and Private Land are given equal legal protection and that land ownership is provided for all Liberians, regardless of identity, custom, ethnicity, tribe, language, gender, or otherwise. The customary land of ethnic communities such as the Kpelle, Bassa, Grebo, Gio, Mano, Kru, Lorma, Krahn, Kissi, Mandingo, Vai, Gola, Gbandi, Mende, Sapo, Belle, Dey, and other Africans is declared to be

[119] See Clause 28 of the Bill.

[120] For analysis of Liberian law prior to the Land Rights Act 2018 see the following Rosch (2019); Budy (2018).

communal property[121] that makes up approximately 46% of Liberia's rural land mass.[122] These communities are declared to have corporate personality.[123] Communal property entitles the community to transfer portions of the land through a lease and a right to exclude others and manage the improvements to the land. Members of the community have the authority to govern the land when they act collectively and, by a majority vote of two-thirds, can approve the sale, lease, or transfer of community land to non-members of the community.[124]

Community members appoint a Community Land Development and Management Committee (CLMDC) to manage customary land on behalf of the community. Membership in the CLMDC is an equal representation of men, women, and youth. Community chiefs shall be ex-officio members, and CLMDC decisions shall be made by consensus.

Communal land is not to be sold or permanently alienated until 2068, except in the case of the residences of community members[125] which, as noted above, is automatic. The CLMDC supervises the automatic transfer of exclusive ownership of members' residential land to the member if the residence was active at the commencement of the Act. In addition, customary land can be leased according to the customs, traditions, and practices of the community. Article 68 allows community members to mortgage a part or the whole of their residential area to secure the payment of a debt or the performance of any obligation.

The overriding power of the community over its lands is recognised by Article 34(4): 'The Community shall not deprive a Community Member of his or her Residential Area. Any restriction on the exercise of the Land rights of a Community Member shall not be valid except it is in accordance with the customs and traditions of the Community and are not in violation of the provisions of this Act and the Constitution of Liberia, provided that the Community shall compensate a Community Member with comparable Land when Land is taken from a Community Member by the Community'.

[121] See https://www.cia.gov/the-world-factbook/countries/liberia/.

[122] See https://www.cia.gov/the-world-factbook/countries/liberia/.

[123] Article 35(2) as above.

[124] See Art 36 of the Land Rights Act.

[125] See Art 49.

2.6 Sierra Leone

Sierra Leone's Customary Land Rights Act 2022 (CLRA 2022) is the culmination of decades of land reform.[126] The total land mass of Sierra Leone is populated by the following ethnic groups: Temne, Mende, Limba, Kono, Korankoh, Fullah, Mandingo, Loko, Sherbro, Creole, and others.

All customary land rights are defined as the full range of primary rights (the right to exclude, transfer, transact, bequeath, manage, and make decisions about the land) and secondary rights (rights of way, access to use natural resources, right to drive cattle, right to obtain water from a river) to land under customary law are collectively owned under family and community titles in Sierra Leone and also individually owned.

Family and community members have usufructuary rights on family and community land. Families are entitled to enter a written land transaction under customary law if agreed to by the head of the family and at least 60% of male and female family members. The written document of land transaction must be approved by the Chiefdom Council Committee for certification, after which it is forwarded to the District Registry for registration. The land transactions envisaged by the CLRA 2022 include seasonal, indefinite, short-term, and long-term tenancies recognised under customary law.[127] A long-term tenancy cannot exceed 50 years, and an option to renew for a term not exceeding 21 years is prohibited. Indefinite tenancies are prohibited. A written customary pledge is another recognised land transaction. The CLRA 2022 guarantees that all Sierra Leonean citizens, irrespective of ethnic restrictions, as well as other social factors, such as gender, religion, age, marital status, social status, and economic status, can enter into written customary tenancies and pledges. The family and community are recognised agents of collective land transactions and have been mandated to use such lands for wealth creation on behalf of the family and the community. Safeguards for foreign investments are set out in Section 26 of the CLRA 2022 and include a maximum duration of 50 years, minimum shareholding participation of 10% in the foreign company, and maximum size of 15,000,10,000, and 5000 hectares for agricultural, mining, and other purposes, respectively. A fair representation of the community must agree to a foreign investment in community land, while it is at least six male and female members for family land. The written informed consent of community members in the form of certified minutes must accompany a certified lease agreement containing agreed and statutory terms to be submitted to the District Land Commission for registration.

Following customary law, communal and family members can transform their collective titles to individual titles that allow them to deal with their land as they deem fit. The elaborate framework for family and communal land leases suggests that Sierra Leone prefers collective engagements with local and foreign investors to

[126] See the following literature for a history of land reform in Sierra Leone, see Ryan (2024), Unruh (2008).

[127] See sect 15 of the CLRA 2022.

address the reasons for indigenous land reform while promoting the family and community crucial to indigenous land tenure.

2.7 *Tanzania*

Tanzanian citizens are entitled to own customary rights of occupancy granted by the Village Council in terms of the Village Land Act 1999.[128] The privatisation of indigenous land tenure is contemplated by the fundamental principles of National Land Policy, set out in Section 3 of the Village Land Act, and include the objectives to recognise that all land in Tanzania is public land vested in the President as trustee on behalf of all citizens to undertake several functions including to ensure that existing rights and recognised long-standing occupation or use of land are clarified and secured by the law; to facilitate an equitable distribution of, and access to, land by all citizens; to regulate the amount of land that any one person or corporate body may occupy or use; to ensure that land is used productively in accordance with the principles of sustainable development; and to facilitate the operation of a market in land; to regulate the operation of a market in land so as to ensure that rural and urban small-holders and pastoralists are not disadvantaged, in case of land to be used for pastoral purposes, use the land in a sustainable manner in accordance with the highest and best customary principles of pastoralism practised in the area.

Village land is held subject to certain conditions including the consent of the Village Council before any buildings are erected; payment of any rent, fees, charges, taxes and other required payments, and with compliance with all rules, including all rules of customary law and all bylaws applicable to the land and all lawful orders and directions by the village council or any person acting with the authority of the village council relating to his use and occupation of the land or any orders of any local or other authority having jurisdiction over land in the area where the land is situated or any orders of any officer exercising powers under this Act.

A person, family, or group of persons, may apply to the Village Council in accordance with Section 22 of the Village Land Act that should result in a written offer setting out the terms and conditions of the proposed grant of the right of occupancy. If the offer is accepted, the Village Council proceeds to grant the right of occupancy by issuing a certificate of occupancy that is also to be signed, sealed, and registered by the District Land Officer.[129] The length of a term of occupancy may be for an indefinite or definite term and is open to all Tanzanian citizens. The conditions that attach to occupancy rights are set out in Section 29 of the TVA and include that the occupier will use and will take steps to ensure that those persons occupying and working the land will: (i) keep and maintain the land in a good state and (ii) in the case of land to be used for agriculture, farm the land in accordance with the practice

[128] Chapter 114 as amended up to 2019. Hereafter 'TVA'.

[129] Section 25 of the TVA.

of good husbandry, customarily used in the area. The status of a customary right of occupancy is of equal status and effect to a granted right of occupancy; it can be inherited or transmitted by will and governed by customary law, including rules of succession. Section 20 further clarifies the customary law that is applicable to a customary right of occupancy by voiding any customary law rule that denies women, children, and persons with disability lawful access to ownership occupation and use of the land.

Tanzania's Village Act recognises the right of holders of customary occupancy rights to create customary leases and sub-leases licences; a usufructuary right as well as similar rights on approval of the Village Council.[130] The disposition of derivative rights by holders of a certificate or rights of occupancy must be approved by the Village Council.[131] However, small mortgages are exempted.

The right of the Village Council to impose remedies available to customary law,[132] such as a fine,[133] and temporarily assign the customary right of occupancy for breach of a condition to the grant of a customary right of occupancy improves the Council's ability to promote indigenous law and ensure that the privatisation of individual tenure proceeds within that framework. It is refreshing that the imposition of remedies in accordance with customary law is to follow due process starting from information of the breach to the person alleged to have breached the condition and the opportunity to make representations on the matter before determining the remedy.[134]

The Tanzanian Village Act is another example of state ownership of land, but with significant recognition of indigenous land tenure. This legislation recognises the occupation and use of village land by villagers in accordance with the applicable customary law.[135] State control of land in Tanzania is vested in the state, and the legislative affirmation of this fact is not surprising since the Tanzanian constitution recognises state ownership of all Tanzanian lands. In turn, members of villages, families in villages, a group of two or more citizens, whether associated under any law or a partnership or a corporate body with majority of members as citizens, can be granted a customary right of occupancy.[136]

Tanzania's Village Council manages village land as a trust and exercises its functions like a trustee.[137] The principles of sustainable development and consultation with stakeholders and beneficiaries of the trust guide the Council.

---

[130] See sect 2 of the TVA

[131] See for example sects 31 32 and 33 of the TVA which provides the process for the creation of a customary lease and sub-lease.

[132] See sect38(1)(A) of the TVA.

[133] Ibid. sect 38(1)(b).

[134] See sect 39 of the TVA.

[135] See sect 7(7)(c) of the TVA.

[136] See sect 14 and 18(1)(a) of the TVA.

[137] See sect 8 of the TVA.

3 State Ownership and Privatised Indigenous Land Tenure

A second framework of indigenous land tenure is a tenure that consists of rights of use of indigenous tenure where land is vested with the state. Since ownership of all land is vested with the state, all other uses by communities and individuals are rights of use. Whether and how indigenous land tenure survives state appropriation of land is an ongoing challenge. The nature of the customary land holding that is available to members of indigenous communities is also a matter of construction if privatisation means the capacity of members of an indigenous community to deal with land without reference to their indigenous community.

An appropriate question is whether the vesting of land in the state diminishes the character of indigenous land tenure. In other words, can indigenous land tenure exist where communities are not the owners of the land? It appears that a tentative answer is positive as long as certain communal incidents of ownership are recognised as derivatives of the state's radical title.

Several African countries recognise state ownership of indigenous land tenure directly and indirectly. Angola and Mozambique expressly affirm state ownership of land, including indigenous land.

3.1 Mozambique

Mozambique, which is made up of the following ethnic groups including the Makhuwa, Tsonga, Lomwe, Sena, Mestizo, and others, including European, Indian, Pakistani, and Chinese, also recognises state ownership of land[138] but does not specifically recognise communal land tenure. It should be noted that Article 111 of the Constitution directs the state to protect rights acquired through inheritance and occupation, suggesting some indirect protection of indigenous land tenure.

Article 3 of the 1997 Mozambique Land Law declares that land is the property of the state and cannot be sold or otherwise alienated, mortgaged, or encumbered. Citizens of Mozambique have the right to private interests in land within the framework of state ownership of land. These private interests, known as *DUAT*, are the right to land use and benefit for a maximum of 100 years, after which a renewal can be sought.[139] The limited term does not extend to personal residential use and family use. The right to land use and benefit is acquired by occupancy in accordance with customary norms and practices, or by at least a good-faith ten-year occupation, or by acquisition through the approval of an application for such right. Holders of the right to land use and benefits have a right to transfer improvements on the land,

---

[138] See Arts 109 and 110 of the Constitution of the Republic of Mozambique 2004, as revised up to 2018.

[139] See Arti 10 of the Mozambique Land Law.

including using the infrastructure as security for a mortgage.[140] But they cannot mortgage the land over which they have a DUAT.[141] The ability of citizens to mortgage the improvements of their land can be described as a limited privatisation that occurs outside any significant involvement of their indigenous law system. Indeed, academic commentators have pointed out that land reform in Mozambique was designed to achieve tenure security and promote economic investment.[142]

Indeed, Mozambique's land law recognises a customary *DUAT* for communities that occupy land governed by customary law. The ability of citizens to privatise a customary *DUAT* is not supported by legislation and may be unnecessary since these citizens may obtain their *DUAT* through customary inheritance or occupation. Whatever 'limited privatisation' of communal land occurs is at the discretion and with the consent of traditional authorities that manage tenure relations.[143]

Although academic commentary recognises debates about the possibility of abandoning the prohibition of the privatisation of land in the future Mozambique constitutional review remains an issue.[144]

In summation, Mozambique's land tenure is an example of nationalised privatisation, which also recognises indigenous land tenure. The survival of indigenous law is guaranteed in these communities.

3.2 Angola

Angola consists of various ethnic groups including the Ovimbundu, Kimbundu, Bakongo, Mestico (mixed European and native African), and Europeans, along with others predominantly found in urban areas. Angola recognises state ownership of land with significant provision for indigenous law and privatisation.

Article 3 of the 2010 Angolan Constitution[145] recognises the sovereignty of the Angolan state over land. Article 5 of that Constitution recognises that land which is the property of the state may be transferred to individuals. Article 98 recognises the right to private ownership of land. The use of land by local communities is also recognised by Article 5, as is Article 92 of the same Constitution that enjoins the state to recognise and protect the right of rural communities to use and benefit from means of production which include land. Articles 15 and 98 of the Angolan Constitution of 2010 declare that land is the property of the state and further

[140] Ibid. Art 16.

[141] See for example, Ghebru and others (2015).

[142] See for example, Hull, Whittall (2018), pp. 2–117; Van den Brink (2008), pp. 1–4.

[143] See De Sousa Santos (2006), pp. 59–75.

[144] See De Quadros.

[145] As amended up to 2021.

recognise access to and use of land by local communities through land rights, which are also recognised by Article 37(2).[146]

Article 9 of the 2004 Angolan Land Law recognises the land rights of rural communities that are defined as:

> communities of neighboring or cohabiting families that, in rural areas, have collective rights to possession, administration, use and fulfillment of the means of community production, namely, of the rural community lands occupied by them and worked in a useful and effective manner according to the principles of self administration and governance, whether for their habitation, for the exercise of their activities, or even for the effecting of other ends recognized by custom and by the present document or its regulations.

A reading of Article 37 and Article 63(4) of the Angolan Land Law of 2004 protects the land rights of rural communities[147] from concessions except when rural communities use the land as security for a loan. There is a recognition of private land rights in Angola's urban and rural areas through the operation of Articles 38, 39, and 40.

In sum, the recognition of individual land holding and the indigenous land tenure of rural communities as features of Angolan land jurisprudence ensures that they exist concurrently. There are reports of extensive expropriation of rural land for agricultural and industrial purposes,[148] suggesting that individual lands are not subject to communal land tenure, and also that indigenous land tenure is steadily being diminished.

3.3 *Nigeria*

Nigeria has a total land mass of 923,768 km^2 with the following ethnic groups: Hausa, Yoruba, Igbo (Ibo) Fulani, Tiv, Kanuri/Beriberi, Ibibio, Ijaw/Izon, and other smaller ethnic nationalities. Nigeria's population is roughly equally divided between urban and rural areas. As the analysis in chapter "An Overview of Indigenous Land Tenure in Africa" of this book reveals, colonial and post-colonial Nigerian courts recognised the privatisation of indigenous land tenure. By the time Nigeria's significant land tenure reform unfolded through the Land Use Act, Nigerians could acquire indigenous land tenure through family and communal sale of this tenure. Since the Land Use Act recognises that all land, including customary rights of occupancy, is vested in the state, it was thought that indigenous land tenure was threatened for a while. There were statutory hints that indigenous land tenure was still recognised because Section 36 of the Land Use Act acknowledged customary rights of

[146] Article 37(2) provides that: 'The state shall respect and protect the property and any other rights in rem of private individuals, corporate bodies and local communities, and temporary civil requisition and expropriation for public use shall only be permitted upon prompt payment of just compensation under the terms of the Constitution and the law.'

[147] See Orani and Schemers (2017).

[148] See for example Amnesty International (2019).

occupancy in respect of land in a non-urban area, which was, immediately before the commencement of this Act, held or occupied by any person. Such occupier or holder of land, whether under customary rights or otherwise, shall, if that land was on the commencement of this Act being used for agricultural purposes, continue to be entitled to possession of the land for use for agricultural purposes as if a customary right of occupancy had been granted to the occupier or holder thereof by the appropriate local government.

Other aspects of the Land Use Act reinforce the existence and strength of land tenure privatisation. State ownership enables the privatisation of indigenous land tenure because Nigeria's local governments and the state Governor can grant customary rights of occupancy over indigenous land tenure. Since these pieces of indigenous land tenure belong to indigenous communities, the power of compulsory acquisition has been a ready tool to dispossess indigenous communities. This fact was acknowledged by the Nigerian Supreme Court in *Abioye v Yakubu*,[149] where the Court held that Section 36 of the Act relating to agricultural holding, even though explaining limited holding per individual, has not divested the traditional holders of their land unless such land is legally acquired by the government or local authority. In *Ogunola v Eiyekole*,[150] the Nigerian Supreme Court stated that: 'Land is still under customary tenure even though dominium is in the Governor. The most pervasive effect of the Land Use Act is the diminution of the plenitude of powers of the holder of land, the character in which they hold remains substantially the same'.[151] Furthermore, customary certificates of occupancy are stripped of the restrictions of indigenous land tenure so that their owners can exercise the incidents of ownership, as stated in Section 21 of the Land Use Act, which provides that a customary right of occupancy may be alienated by assignment, mortgage, transfer of possession, sublease, or otherwise, with the consent of a Governor or the local government. Pertinent questions include whether customary rights of occupancy can be transferred under the Land Use Act and whether there are incidents of indigenous land tenure binding holders of transferred customary rights of occupancy. The answer to the first question is positive and is supported by a long line of Nigerian cases where absolute titles to indigenous land tenure are recognised through the sale or assignment of land after the enactment of the Land Use Act in 1975, for example in *Agbonifo v Aiwereoba*,[152] *Finnih v Imade*,[153] and *Enabulele v Agbonlahor*,[154] where Nigerian courts have recognised absolute titles to transferred communal and or family indigenous land tenure. This fact is not surprising since, as stated above, the law on land tenure in Nigeria before the LUA recognised the privatisation of

[149] (1991) All NLR 1.

[150] [1990]4 NWLR (Pt 146) 632.

[151] Ibid at p.635.

[152] 1988 1 NWLR (pt 70) 325.

[153] [1982] 1 NWLR (Pt 219) 511.

[154] [1999] 4 NWLR (Pt. 598) 166.

indigenous land tenure subject to the consent rules. In a long line of cases,[155] the principal members of the community and family owners of the land must consent to the sale of the land. It was also the case that the title obtained from the sale of a customary right of occupancy amounted to an absolute interest in land. After the LUA, a double-tier system of consent is now in place. After the consent of the community or family, the consent of the Governor or the Chairman of the Local Government Council with respect to land in an urban or non-urban area, respectively, must be obtained. The seminal case of *Savannah Bank of Nigeria v Ajilo*[156] specifically addressed deemed grants of statutory rights of occupancy similar to deemed rights of customary rights of occupancy which preserve indigenous land tenure to hold that lack of the Governor's consent renders the transaction null and void.[157] The answer to the second question, regarding whether there are incidents of indigenous land tenure that follow the transfer of indigenous land tenure, is nuanced. Cases such as *Abioye v Yakubu*[158] suggest that customary interests in land that predate the Land Use Act may be created with the consent of the Governor and the appropriate local government. Consequently, any grant of a customary right of occupancy does not extinguish existing indigenous land tenure interests in the right of occupancy unless such an interest has been compulsorily acquired. Customary interests in contemplation here include customary tenancies and customary pledges. In both examples, conflicts of land use that arise because of the customary incidents of such interests are resolved by indigenous law. For example, whether the use of a piece of land covered by a customary tenancy for an unintended purpose could lead to a forfeiture of such tenancy, as decided in cases such as *Ehimare v Emhonyon*,[159] is resolved through principles of indigenous law. The same point applies to the challenge of the title of an overlord by a customary tenant, such as in the case of *Onah v Onyia.*[160] In the same light, principles of indigenous law are used to determine the existence and features of customary pledges that are indigenous mortgages. For example, customary mortgages are perpetually redeemable following decisions in cases such as *Agada Ekoiko v Esedalue.*[161]

The management of customary rights of occupancy is entrusted to a statutory authority, namely the Land Allocation Advisory Committee established by Section 2(5) of the Land Use Act, and not to traditional authorities that, in a sense, were believed to assist in decoupling indigenous land from traditional authorities. These Committees have had a modest, if not negligible, effect on traditional authorities if the Nigerian land market is a useful measure.[162]

---

[155] See for example, Alao v Ajani (1989) 4 NWLR Pt. 113 p. 1.

[156] (1990) 4 NWLR Pt. 146, p. 632.

[157] See the cases of *Salami v Oke* [1987] 4 NWLR (Pt 63) 1.

[158] [1991] 5 NWLR (Pt 190) 130.

[159] (1985) 2 SC 49.

[160] [1989] 1 NWLR (Pt 99) 514.

[161] (1974) 3 SC 15.

[162] See for example, Iwarere (2008).

However, recognising that indigenous land tenure survives the Land Use Act has strengthened traditional authorities in concluding agreements to dispose of indigenous land tenure. For example, the indigenous law-sanctioned procedure for acquiring indigenous law has been sanctioned by Nigerian courts. For example, in *Agbonifo v Aiwereoba*,[163] the Nigerian Supreme Court distilled principles of a valid grant of customary land amongst the Bini people of Nigeria. It stands to reason that the grant of consent by the Governor or the appropriate local government in contravention of indigenous law principles could be a ground for impugning such traditional transfers.

In summary, Nigeria's Land Use Act is another example of nationalised land privatisation in the sense that it formalised decades of individual user rights within state ownership. The tenure of indigenous land continues in existence and in support of indigenous communities. Conveyancing practices in the Nigerian land market have turned the rights of occupancies into *de facto* freehold titles and reflect economic pressures on indigenous land tenure for economically viable titles.[164]

3.4 Botswana

The transfer of land administration from Botswana's indigenous chiefs to Land Boards and the rights of all Batswana citizens to own tribal land irrespective of ethnic affiliation define Botswana's indigenous land tenure as unique. The country's land is divided into tribal land, state land or freehold land. Ng'ong'ola[165] estimates that tribal land covers approximately 71% of Botswana's land mass, state land is approximately 23%, and freehold land is approximately 5%. At the time of Botswana's independence, tribal land was recognised as belonging to the different ethnic groups and managed and used by customary law. The nomenclature of these lands as 'tribal' is with reference to their origin as land 'previously occupied and utilised by indigenous communities under various customary laws and practices'.[166]

All tribal land in Botswana is symbolically vested in the people of Botswana and is managed on their behalf by Tribal Land Boards that were first established by the 1968 Tribal Land Act and the 2018 Tribal Land Act. The Land Boards function like body corporates with perpetual succession and with significant state control that can give directions to the Board. A quasi-state status of the Board is also buttressed by the functions of the Board, as well as the appointment and removal by the Minister in charge of Lands. For example, the Tribal Land Act is composed of 11 members, 8 of whom are appointed by the Minister of Lands. Although a tribal chief is an

163 1988 1 NWLR (pt 70) 325.

164 See, for example, Oshio (1989), pp. 19–30.

165 Ng'ong'ola (2017), pp. 113–139. See generally Ng'ong'ola (1992), pp. 140–167; Ng'ong'ola (1996), pp. 1–29; Ng'ong'ola (1997), pp. J1–26; and Morolong and Ng'ong'ola (2007), pp. 142–175.

166 See Ng'ong'ola (2019), pp. 3–35.

ex-officio member, the appointment is unrelated to the traditional authority over a tribal area. By establishing the Tribal Land Board, the 1968 Tribal Land Act removed the management of control of land from tribal chiefs while retaining customary land tenure. The 2018 Tribal Land Act[167] continues this trend by reaffirming the authority and jurisdiction of 12 Land Boards in the country, with control of tribal areas constituting approximately 70% of Botswana's land mass.[168]

As stated above, Section 23 of the 2018 Tribal Land Act recognises private interests in tribal lands in Botswana in the form of customary land grants or leases available to all citizens of Botswana, irrespective of their ethnic affiliation. Of importance is the fact that Section 23(1) states that the only acceptable evidence of tribal land is a deed of grant of customary land rights issued by the Registrar of Deeds. The evidence of a customary grant in the form of a deed strengthens individual interest in tribal land, further signalling Botswana as a leader in the privatisation of indigenous land tenure in Africa.

A crucial question is whether such privatisation has significantly impacted the strength or otherwise of the indigenous communities of Botswana. To answer the question, several facts should be noted. First, it is clear that indigenous land tenure continues in operation in the form of norms, values, and institutions that govern tribal land. There is no extinguishment of these facts, and even if there were such an abolition of the indigenous framework, indigenous tenurial law would still thrive. Second, all Batswana, irrespective of ethnic affiliation, can be allocated land in any part of Botswana. This decoupling of ethnic affiliation should ordinarily dent the social control of tribal authorities. This is not a likely scenario because it is in the interests of the non-ethnic Batswana to enjoy the customary tenure in harmony with ethnic Batswana in whose territory this tribal land is located. Customary land rights, such as use, occupation, access, and burial rights, are often meaningful in concert with other pieces of land and occupiers. Third, the 2018 Tribal Land Act recognises the crucial role of tribal authorities in formulating its policy because Section 5(5) imposes a duty of consultation of tribal authorities, and relevant tribal authorities are members of the Land Board. Fourth, Land Boards can impose any restriction on the use of tribal land, which could include fidelity to the indigenous land tenure law. There is considerable support for academic commentators who have argued that the Tribal Land Act of 1968 and by extension the 2018 Act did not change customary land law other than by transferring the authority over land from the chief to the land board.[169] The Land Boards are charged with the grant; cancellation; authorisation of any change of use; authorisation of any transfer of tribal land, and imposition of restrictions on tribal land.[170]

---

[167] The Tribal Land Act 2018 (hereafter TLA 2018) commenced in April 2022.

[168] See Schedule 1 to the Tribal Land Act lists the Tribal Areas in Botswana and the appropriate Tribal Land Board.

[169] See for example, Adams (2003).

[170] See sect 5 of the Tribal Land Act.

The extent to which these customary lands are part of or subject to indigenous affiliation is doubtful, since it can exist to the extent that the Land Boards inscribe indigenous norms, values, and obligations in the grants of tribal land and are upheld by Botswana courts. While succession to tribal land is governed by customary law rules, as seen in the case of *Ngwateske*, individual ownership of tribal land is the cornerstone of the tenurial scheme in Botswana. The consent of the Land Board is required for transfer, mortgage, charge, bond, or lease capable of running for a period of five years or more, exchange, partition, or other disposal or dealing with any tribal land; the division of any such land into two or more parcels to be held under separate titles; or the issue, sale, transfer, mortgage, or any other disposal of, or dealing with, any share in a private company owning any land.

It is now the law that consultation with and consent of an indigenous community is critical in the alienation of tribal land because of a recent majority decision of the Botswana Court of Appeal in *Attorney General of Botswana v Seboko.*[171] The Court of Appeal held that the purported acquisition of part of the Ga-Matele tribal land based on a 1973 amendment to Section 7 of the Tribal Land Act of 1970 amounted to an unconstitutional deprivation of property. The Malate Land Board, on behalf of the Botswana government, argued that this attempt breached Sections 3(c), 8, and 15 of the Botswana Constitution.

The Ga-Matele tribe purchased this land in 1925 to address the shortage of land for grazing purposes. A deed of transfer was registered in the Deeds Registry in favour of the tribe. It is common cause that during Botswana's communal land tenure nationalisation, part of Forest Hill in contention was not part of the land transferred to the Malete Land Board. After the nationalisation process, the Ga-Malete tribe requested the Malete Land Board to manage its property, which continued until 2003, when the tribe resolved to take over the management of this property and registered a trust to that effect. After establishing and commencing the trust, the tribe began negotiations with the government of Botswana for the possible purchase of part of Forest Hill covered by the trust. A High Court matter instituted by the Malete Land Board argued that the deed of transfer in favour of the trust was invalid because the tenure of Botswana's legislative scheme vested the land in question in the Malete Land Board. The High Court and the Court of Appeal agreed with the Ga-Malete tribe that the legislative scheme through which the state assumed ownership of tribal land outside the 1970 legislative schemes amounted to compulsory land acquisition because of the lack of consultation and consent to such takings. The import of the decision of the Botswana Court of Appeal is enhanced protection of the communal land of Batswana indigenous communities.

The fact that consultation and consent of the indigenous community property owner are essential to the validity of a legislative expropriation of property is significant and an improvement to the widely held view that payment of compensation discharges the duty of the state in compulsory acquisition. The decision of the Botswana Court of Appeal is hugely significant as an encouragement to other

[171] Court of Appeal Civil Appeal No. CACGB-153-21 of 7-03-2023.

African judiciaries to find that the consent of indigenous African communities is vital to the validity of all administrative and legislative acquisitions of their property.

3.5 Namibia

It is estimated[172] that 43% of Namibia's land area is held under freehold title by individuals, close corporations, while another 39% of the land is 'communal land'. According to Werner:

> In 2014, just over 40% of Namibia's population of 2 234 million lived in agricultural households in communal areas. The Namibia Census of Agriculture 2013/20142 recorded 169 984 agricultural households, with a total population of 907 715, holding tenure rights to agricultural land in communal areas. Ninety-two per cent of these households lived in the seven northern-central and eastern communal areas in which rainfed cropping and livestock husbandry are the main agricultural activities. Only 8% lived in the other seven regions which rely primarily on extensive livestock farming for their livelihoods …

Namibia, like several other states such as Tanzania, grants ownership of communal land in the state.[173] The idea of privatization, as the existence of individual lands carved out of communal land, is not a feature of Namibian indigenous land tenure. Communal land is a form of indigenous land tenure with members of indigenous communities entitled to private tenure rights to homesteads, cropping fields, and cattle pens in terms of the CLRA.[174] These tenure rights are described by the CLRA as 'commonages' and governed by customary law; it is not surprising that they are informal and do not amount to outright ownership. The CLRA also recognises ordinary leasehold and agricultural leasehold rights as a form of tenure recognised under communal land tenure. The leasehold rights are a response to the clamour for privatisation and alienation. Consequently, Section 30(2) of the CLRA requires the Minister, after consultation with a relevant Communal Land Board and Traditional Authority, to designate an area where an agricultural leasehold may be granted. Werner believes that these leaseholds aim:

'to promote economic development in the communal areas by enabling farmers to obtain long-term leases over their land which can be registered in the Deeds Office. This, it is assumed, will enable them to use their land as collateral to raise loans for agricultural development'.[175]

---

[172] See for example, Werner (2021).

[173] See sect 17 of the Communal Land Reform Act (CLRA) provides that: '… all communal land areas vest in the State in trust for the benefit of the traditional communities residing in those areas and to promote the economic and social development of the people of Namibia, in particular the landless and those with insufficient access to land who are not in formal employment or engaged in non-agriculture business activities. See also Article 16 of the Namibian Constitution.'

[174] See sect 15 of the Communal Land Reform Act.

[175] Werner (2021), p. 35.

Communal land tenure is managed thoroughly by communal land boards and traditional authorities that ensure that indigenous law is applied, protected, and respected. A Traditional Authority is determined by the Traditional Authorities Act 2000 and exercises the powers of the community in the allocation and cancellation of customary land rights except agricultural leaseholds. Traditional Authorities determine the use of grazing land, including foreigners' access to such land. The right to allocate customary land rights by Section 30 of the CLRA is first made by the Chief of a Traditional Authority in whose communal area the land is situated, in consultation with members of the Traditional Authority. The Traditional Authorities Act 2000 recognises the right of Traditional Authorities to administer and execute the customary law of that traditional community, as well as uphold, protect, and preserve the culture, language, tradition, and traditional values of that community, as well as make customary laws. In particular, appeals against the exercise of the powers of a Traditional Authority to consent to the transfer of a customary land right or any other exercise of customary law by a Traditional Authority recognised in Section 39 of the CLRA should have a calming effect on a Traditional Authority and is in line with regulatory mechanisms across Africa that subject the exercise of indigenous law to external agencies must be for the benefit renewal and sustenance of indigenous law.

Communal Land Boards are charged with exercising control over the allocation and cancellation of customary land rights by Chiefs or Traditional Authorities, approving applications for a right of leasehold, as well as establishing and maintaining a register and a system of registration for recording the allocation, transfer, and cancellation of customary land rights and rights of leasehold. The membership of the Communal Land Boards includes four women, one representative of Traditional Authorities in the Board's area of operations, one person representing the organised farming community, and the regional office. In addition, there are four staff members of the public service. The membership and functions of Communal Land Boards suggest a democratisation of the exercise of indigenous law and authority. The requirement for the consent of the Land Board to the transfer of leaseholds is certain to facilitate the use of such leaseholds for purposes that have driven the privatisation of indigenous land tenure in Africa.

3.6 Ethiopia

Current estimates show that Ethiopia's population is more than 120 million people with a land mass of 1,109,800 km^2 of which more than 80% of the population lives in rural areas. Ethiopia is generally conceived of as a highland and lowland dichotomy. In the highland area, which constitutes about a quarter of the land mass, many Ethiopians live in the rural areas. The lowlands of Ethiopia consist of the majority of pastoral land holdings of indigenous communities, predominantly in the Afar, Somali, Oromiya, Southern Nations Nationalities and Peoples' (SNPP), Tigray,

Benishangul-Gumz and Gambella States.[176] Abdullahi describes the socio-economic and cultural systems of pastoral communities as based on communality, and that land is:

> [H]eld traditionally under the collective possession and ownership of their community. Their communal land tenure arrangements have traditional rules and regulations that aim at harmonising ecological, economic and social benefit.[177]

Indigenous law, therefore, governs the communal tenure of Ethiopia's pastoral communities and represents the normative framework of what Ethiopian constitutional property jurisprudence refers to as 'communal land'. Whether indigenous law is recognised under the Ethiopian constitution is doubted by some commentators, although it is clear that the recognition of nations, peoples, and communities by Article 39 of Ethiopia's Constitution necessarily approves that the normative framework of these communities is recognised.

Many commentators understand Ethiopian land tenure in three historical epochs.[178] The first period is the Feudal period, where the Ethiopian monarchy owned and controlled all land in the country. With user rights granted to citizens, the land eventually became family land. The second period is the Derg period, during which the Ethiopian military regime nationalised all land but recognised a user right for all Ethiopians. Under the present constitutional dispensation, the Federal Democratic Republic of Ethiopia recognises indigenous tenure within a constitutional context that recognises private property. Thus, while Article 39 of the Constitution provides that every nation, nationality, and people has the right to speak, to write, and to develop its own language; to express, to develop, and to promote its culture; and to preserve its history, the right to private property is recognised by Article 40 of the Federal Constitution that provides that the right to ownership of rural and urban land, as well as of all natural resources, is exclusively vested in the state and in the peoples of Ethiopia. Article 40(3) further provides that land is a common property of the nations, nationalities, and peoples of Ethiopia and shall not be subject to sale or other means of exchange. Article 40(5) declares that Ethiopian pastoralists have the right to free land for grazing and cultivation, as well as the right not to be displaced from their possession. It must be noted that there are commentators who argue that these constitutional provisions do not recognise communal land tenure.[179]

The constitutional context of the recognition of indigenous tenure is further defined by the power to enact laws for the utilisation and conservation of land and other natural resources in the country and is exclusively given to the federal government by Article 51(5) of the Constitution obligating regional governments—Afar, Amhara, Benishangul-Gumuz, Gambela, Harari, Oromia, Somali, the Southern Nations, Nationalities, and Peoples' Region, Tigray, Sidama, and South West

[176] See generally Abdullahi (2007), pp. 85–125.

[177] Above p. 90.

[178] See for example, Agegnehu and Mansberger (2020).

[179] See for example, Abdo (2014), p. 204.

Ethiopia—with the duty to administer land and other natural resources according to federal laws.[180]

The Rural Land Administration and Land Use Proclamation 2005 provides a framework for indigenous land tenure in Ethiopia around a user right for all citizens. Article 17(1) of the Act gives regional governments the ability[181] to enact rural land administration and land use laws and provides a framework for the implementation of the principles of the 2005 proclamation. These principles are organised around the acknowledgement of the existence of communal land defined as part of rural land given to local residents for common grazing, forestry, and other social services. Rural land itself is defined as 'land outside of a municipality'. The first principle is that peasant farmers/pastoralists engaged in agriculture for a living shall be given free rural land without any time limit.[182] Second, any citizen of the country who is 18 years of age or older and wants to engage in agriculture for a living shall have the right to use rural land without any time limit.[183] Third, any person who is a family member of a peasant farmer, semi-pastoralist, or pastoralist having the right to use rural land may obtain rural land from their family by donation, inheritance, or from the competent authority.[184] Fourth, peasant farmers, semi-pastoralists, and pastoralists who are given holding certificates can lease or enter into development activities with other farmers or investors, for a period to be determined by rural land administration laws of regions based on particular local conditions.[185] Rural land users owe certain obligations, such as to use and protect the land to allow the construction of irrigation lines, as well as cooperate to measure and survey their land.[186]

Further privatisation of indigenous land tenure in Ethiopia has been changed by the Federal Democratic Republic of Ethiopia Rural Land Administration and Use Proclamation 1324 of 2024. Its intent is evident in parts of the preamble which assert that:

---

[180] Article 52(2)(d) of the Constitution.

[181] The regional states have enacted regional rural land legislations viz: Oromia National Regional State currently enacted proclamation no. 130/2007; Amhara National Regional State has enacted proclamation no. 133/2006; Southern Nation Nationalities and Peoples Region (SNNPR) state enacted currently working proclamation no. 110/2007 and Tigray National Regional State recently enacted proclamation no. 239/2014; Afar Regional State has enacted proclamation no. 49/2009, Benishangul Gumuz Regional State has enacted proclamation no. 85/2010, Gambela Regional State has enacted proclamation no. 185/2011, and the Somali Regional State has enacted proclamation no. 128/2013.

[182] Article 5(1)(a) of the 2005 Proclamation.

[183] Article 5(1)(b).

[184] Article 5(2).

[185] Article 8.

[186] Article 10.

Preamble

WHEREAS, it has become necessary to improve the livelihood of farmers, semipastoralists, and pastoralists at the level of the Country's economic, political, and social development by establishing improved rural land administration and use system that enhance the land property rights of farmers, semi-pastoralists, and pastoralists over their landholding;

WHEREAS, it has been proved that the customary land use and land management of semi-pastoralists and pastoralists have significant and noticeable importance; and the landholding rights of these groups are recognized under the FDRE Constitution, and it has become necessary to issue laws that implement international and regional treaties to which Ethiopia is signatory.

The 2024 Proclamation sets out three types of rural land holdings as private, communal, and state holdings. The land holding right of farmers, pastoralists, and religious institutions[187] is declared to be a holding right that is defined to include the rights of use, lease, sharecrop, collateralise, joint development, bequeath, donate, transfer through sale or in any form properties fixed on the holding, consolidate, exchange with similar rural land holding, and cultivate the land through cluster arrangement. In addition, rural landholders can lease out their land holdings for a specific period in terms of Article 9. These land holding rights deepen the privatisation of rural land in Ethiopia and are further elaborated in the Proclamation in terms of sharecropping (Article 13); joint development (Article 14); use of land as collateral (Article 15), to mention a few. There are no restrictions on rural holdings by the proclamations that recognise communal land separately, although Article 37 of the Proclamation requires regional laws on land tenure to recognise customary institutions, customary land use and management practices, and conflict resolution mechanisms of pastoral communities. This recognition is conditioned on conformity with fundamental constitutional rights, women's rights, and other rights and obligations. Related questions include whether private rural land ownership precludes customary law. It is plausible that the land use restrictions imposed on rural land use in Article 32 of the Proclamation are a substitute for the principles of customary law which would ordinarily apply to rural land.

Article 24 of the Proclamation sets out the conditions of the recognition of communal land tenure to include a regional law as a framework for communal land tenure, the conferment of legal personality on communities, and a communal landholding certificate. There appears to be a unique recognition of the communal nature of pastoral communities because Section 6 of the 2024 Proclamation is dedicated to Pastoral Land Administration and Use. Article 35 encourages regional states with pastoral communities to issue pastoral communal land administration and use laws. Article 36 prohibits the partition and privatisation of communal land tenure except otherwise decided by these communities. Pastoralist communities can lease communal land tenure if supported by a decision of three-quarters of the user

[187] See Arts 7 and 8 of the 2024 Proclamation.

community and shall not result in the deprivation of grazing land.[188] Such a restriction is an example of a customary easement that would run with the leased land. It is appropriate that the pastoral community may generally subject the leased land to customary land use policies along the lines set out in Article 32 of the 2024 Proclamation. Regions are required to establish a regional Communal Land Users Fund to hold income from communal land, including rent, compensation, sales of any produce from the land and others for the benefit of the community, and special support to economically disadvantaged women and vulnerable groups.[189]

It is to the regional state rural land proclamation that we turn to to discover how the relationship operates between communal land and individual land in the context of the rights to communal land and private property, which are set out above. In general, there are two interlocking principles. First, these state rural land laws recognise the immemorial[190] and communal nature of pastoral lands,[191] because they define communal holding as rural land which is held by two or more persons who have indivisible right over the land and that is used equally by the communal holders. Second, there is the recognition according to the Ethiopian Constitution of the user rights of members of these communities to pastoral land.[192] Accordingly, pastoral land is not to be used for collateral purposes[193] and must not be turned into private holdings beyond the capacity of members of the community to inherit the user rights of their family lineage.[194]

Thus, it is clear that the Ethiopian constitutional property jurisprudence does not easily contemplate the privatisation of pastoral land. However, the sanctity of pastoral land is enhanced by the access of Ethiopians to user rights in rural land. Several commentators argue that the nature of the user rights does not provide security for investment in land.[195] However, like other state-owned land tenures, the recognition

---

[188] See Art 38 of the 2024 Proclamation.

[189] Se Art 39.

[190] See Art 5(1) of the Afar Law: 'The right of pastoralists of the region to use their grazing lands has no time limit.'

[191] Article 8(5). Communal pastoral lands used communally by pastoralists shall not be transferred into private holdings.

[192] Article 5(5) of the Afar Law provides that: 'A person who is the age of IS and above has the right to free access to farm lands where such person intends to engage in sedentary farming and submit his request to the competent authority in the Region.' Article 5(6) of the Afar State Law further provides that: 'Pastoralists have the right to voluntarily settle as sedentary farmers under resettlement programs that may be organized by the Regional Government.'

[193] Article 5 (9). Communal lands that are used communally by pastoralists for grazing, and social services shall not be given/leased to investors. This, however, shall not affect the power of the government, as owner of all lands, to transfer communal holdings into private holdings as deemed necessary and in consultation and in agreement with pastoralists.

[194] Article 5(4) of the Afar State Law provides in this regard that: 'Land holders who have land holdings within the communal land tenure may bequeath their individual land holdings to their children or other legal heirs.'

[195] See for example, Chigbu, Alemayehu and others (2019), pp. 371–383.

of communal land tenure and user rights of Ethiopians reinforces the hold of indigenous law.[196]

3.7 Zimbabwe

Zimbabwe is a vast country of 390,757 km^2 inhabited by Shona, Ndebele, and other peoples such as the Chewa, Chibarwe, Kalanga' Khoisan, Nambya, Ndau, Shangani, Sotho, Tsonga, Tswana, Venda, and Xhosa. Zimbabwe is another country in which the ownership of communal land is vested in the state by the president of the country, through Section 4 of the Communal Land Act. The president has powers to permit the occupation and utilisation of communal land in accordance with the Communal Land Act.[197] Like many countries with title to land vested in the state or the president, Zimbabwean citizens have user rights for agricultural and residential use of communal land.

The Communal Land Act establishes two systems of land allocation in communal land. Section 8 regulates the occupation and use of communal land for agricultural or residential purposes, subject to the consent of the Rural District Council established for the area concerned. The consent of the Rural District Council to occupy and use communal land by any person is premised on several considerations. First, the Councils must have regard to customary law relating to the allocation, occupation, and use of land in the area concerned, and consult and cooperate with the chief appointed to preside over the community concerned in terms of the Traditional Leaders Act. The persons to whom occupation rights are granted must be members of or persons sanctioned by the customary law of communities that have traditionally and continuously occupied and used the land. The Constitutional Court in *Chikutu* has held that the customs of a community take precedence when the local authority is making decisions affecting the community itself.

The second type of user rights are occupational permits issued by Section 9 of the Communal Land Act for administrative purposes of the state or a local or similar authority; religious or educational purposes in the interests of inhabitants of the area concerned; hospitals, clinics, or other such establishments for the benefit of inhabitants of the area concerned; hotels, shops, or other business premises and any other purpose whatsoever which, in the opinion of the rural district council, is in the interests of inhabitants of the area concerned.

Congruent with the dominant communal tenure model in Africa, the Zimbabwean communal land tenure system does not recognise rural land sales and rental markets.[198] The Communal Land Act prohibits the sale of communal land by individuals

[196] See Gebreamanuel (2011), pp. 1–31.

[197] See *Livison Chikutu v Minister of Lands, Agriculture, Water, Climate, and Rural Resettlement* [2023] ZWCC 11. Hereafter *Chikutu*.

[198] Chimhowu and Woodhouse (2006), p. 346.

without the approval of the village head,[199] and it must be converted to state land as confirmed by the Zimbabwean Constitutional Court in *Chikutu.* The case suggests another possibility of privatising indigenous land tenure, which is by the process of expropriation under Section 6 of the Communal Land Act, by which communal land is turned into state land and members of the indigenous communities may seek this state land in their private capacity.[200] It is possible that if allowed by customary law, usufructuary or secondary rights may be transferred with the consent of other adult clan members and the Rural District Council.[201] The Zimbabwean courts have, in cases such as *Chihoro v Rusere*[202] and *Runganga v Nyamangara,*[203] adjudicated the transfer of users' rights and emphasised that such transfers must conform to indigenous law. Accordingly, a permanent alienation of a user's right is only possible with the consent of family members.

The Traditional Leaders Act also regulates the allocation of communal land through the functions of the office of a chief as the traditional head of the community under his jurisdiction. The chiefs who are responsible for ensuring compliance with the Communal Lands Act that includes seeking approvals for transfer of usufructuary rights have continued to allocate communal land without the approval of the Rural District Council, leading to land conflicts.[204]

An analysis of the provisions of Sections 8 and 26 of the Communal Land Act and the Traditional Leaders Act, respectively, reveals the tension between customary and state law in land allocations. While both Sections 8 and 26 of the Communal Land Act and the Traditional Leaders Act, respectively, recognise Rural District Councils as the administrative authority with ultimate control over the use and allocation of all communal land, the sections do not expressly oust the application of customary law. There is ambiguity on the application of customary law in land allocations. By the word 'shall', Section 8 of the Communal Land Act makes it mandatory for Rural District Councils to consider customary law 'relating to the allocation, occupation and use of land in the area concerned'. Additionally, it is mandatory for Rural District Councils to 'consult and co-operate with the chief appointed to preside over the community concerned'. Furthermore, it is mandatory for Rural District Councils to:

[199] See sect 26(3) of the Traditional Leaders Act.

[200] See sect 6(3) of the Communal Land Act.

[201] See sect 28(2) of the Traditional Leaders Act.

[202] [2011] ZWHHC 7.

[203] [2024] ZWCHHC 1.

[204] See the following literature Ncube (2011), p. 89.

> grant consent only to persons who, according to the customary law of the community that has traditionally and continuously occupied and used land in the area concerned, are regarded as forming part of such community or who, according to such customary law, may be permitted to occupy and use such land.[205]

Where no community has traditionally and continuously occupied and used land in the area concerned, the Rural District Council has no power to allocate the land to anyone except to the class of person specified by the Minister of Local Government, Rural, and Urban Development in a notice.

This section should be read together with Section 5 of the Traditional Leaders Act, which sets out the duties of chiefs. The section gives chiefs a broad range of powers over the management of communal land. First, chiefs have the power to ensure that land is allocated in terms of the Communal Land Act. This provision gives the oversight role of land allocations to the chiefs. It is not clear if the legislature intended to create a hierarchical structure in land allocations where Rural District Councils are the administrative authority with the sole power to allocate land, with chiefs having the oversight role. Second, it is the duty of the chiefs to prevent any unauthorised settlement or use of any land under their jurisdiction. Third, it is the role of the chiefs to notify the rural district council of any intended disposal of a homestead and the permanent departure of any inhabitant from his area, and lastly, acting on the advice of the headman, chiefs have the power to approve the settlement of any new settler in their area.

A conflict of laws is inherent in both the Communal Land Act and the Traditional Leaders Act. Rather than resolving the conflict of law between customary rules and statutory rules of land allocation in communal areas, Section 8 of the Communal Land Act, as read with Section 5 of the Traditional Leaders Act, exacerbates the conflict of laws.

The effect of the use of peremptory language in Section 8 of the Communal Land Act is that two systems of law regulate access to communal land without resolving the issue of which legal system prevails in case of conflict of laws. The section conflates the role of chiefs (who apply customary law) and the Rural District Councils (which apply statutory law), thus creating a tension between the application of the two legal systems. In essence, the Communal Land Act requires Rural District Councils (elected local government institutions) to consider customary law (which is a province of traditional leaders) in land allocations. It is left to the imagination what amounts to 'considering customary law'. Furthermore, the Communal Land Act is silent on what is meant by consulting and cooperating with chiefs before allocating land. The Communal Land Act maintains the application of customary law in land allocations while divesting the land allocation powers from traditional leaders to Rural District Councils.

Thus, while purporting to curtail the powers of traditional leaders in land allocations, the Communal Land Act created a dual system of land allocations with

[205] Section 8(2) of the Communal Land Act.

ambiguous powers between the Rural District Councils and the chiefs.[206] Mandondo observes that in practice, traditional leaders remain actively involved in land allocations based on customary and territorial claims to the land.[207]

It is important to note that the Constitution expressly recognises the role of chiefs in the administration of communal land, making it likely that the powers of administration of communal land vest in the traditional authorities under Section 282(1) of the Constitution, traditional leaders are given the function of administering communal land in accordance with an Act of Parliament. Section 282(2) and (3) buttress this position by providing that:

> **Section 282(2) and (3)**
> 2. Except as provided in an Act of Parliament, traditional leaders have authority, jurisdiction and control over the Communal Land or other areas for which they have been appointed, and over persons within those Communal Lands or areas.
>
> 3. In the performance of their functions, traditional leaders are not subject to the direction or control of any person or authority, except as may be prescribed in an Act of Parliament.

The Constitution does not define the word 'administer'. However, the ordinary meaning of the word 'administer' means to manage, to take charge, to carry out a task, or give something to someone.[208] It is pertinent to note that Sections 275 and 276 of the Constitution, which set out the duties of local authorities for rural areas, do not expressly provide for the administration of communal land as a function of Rural District Councils. The constitutional land administrative provisions should be read together with Section 332 of the Constitution, which defines communal land as land held in accordance with customary law by members of a community under the leadership of a Chief. The fact that traditional leaders are given this function by the Constitution means that while an Act of Parliament can limit their administrative powers, it cannot exclude them completely. The conspicuous absence of the mention of Rural District Councils in all constitutional provisions relating to the administration of communal land lends support to the argument that the Constitution envisages a position where traditional leaders, as opposed to local authorities, are administering communal land held in accordance with customary law. As a result, Section 8 of the Communal Land Act and Section 26 of the Traditional Leaders Act, which exclusively vest communal land administration on the Rural District Councils, conflict with the constitutional dictates and are thus unconstitutional.

---

[206] Ncube (2011), p. 90.

[207] Mandondo (2000).

[208] https://www.oxfordlearnersdictionaries.com/definition/american_english/administer Accessed 04-11-2025.

4 An Assessment of the Future of Indigenous Law in Africa through the Models of Privatisation of Indigenous Land Tenure in Africa

The models of privatisation of indigenous land tenure reveal a rich diversity of outcomes given the different iterations of the objective of turning what is essentially a communal land holding into individual ownership, control, and management. Identifying between the two models requires a subtle and contextual engagement in any statutory reform process. Often, the true character of the process becomes evident in the implementation of the reform process. Indeed, African judiciaries have been instrumental in charting a course for the third stage of the reform process, where they have been presented with opportunities to interpret these new laws. For example, the leverage of human rights is a potential game-changer. Furthermore, recent judicial recognition of the rights of women to inherit the tenure of indigenous land significantly improves access to indigenous land tenure for the disadvantaged. In many other instances, indigenous land tenure continues unabated in many respects, perpetuating discrimination and exclusion. Another example is from Nigeria, where the judicial clarification of the status of customary law as continuing even in the face of nationalisation of land in Nigeria has been crucial. The example that is lacking in this regard is the silence on the embedded indigenous law, even on privatised land. The analysis above suggests that there may be no fundamental differences between states where the communal ownership and management of indigenous land tenure is recognised, and states like Tanzania, Mozambique, and Nigeria, which have sought to manage the nationalisation of all land by promoting private interests and communal management of indigenous land tenure. If the idea that indigenous law is inherently adaptable and, where necessary, developed, it is acceptable to conclude that all statutory and constitutional privatisation of indigenous land tenure is normal and to be expected. As highlighted in the previous chapters, individual tenure is no stranger to communal land tenure in Africa and that access rather than ownership is often the foundation of indigenous land tenure in Commonwealth African states. What follows is an assessment that attempts to make sense of the different national legislative and constitutional tenure reforms and their consequences for the future of indigenous law in Africa.

The first point is to ascertain whether there is a uniform idea of privatisation and, more importantly, whether this is possible or desirable. It is important to point out the broad categories of the privatisation of indigenous land tenure and even the wide differences in national approaches to what the term privatisation of indigenous land tenure refers to, beyond the broad understanding that it refers to all instances in which communal land tenure becomes exclusively individual, in the sense that members of indigenous communities are able to deal with their land in an autonomous manner without the community. The simple answer is that such uniformity cannot be discerned, especially as the discussions in this chapter have demonstrated, and that individual interests in communal indigenous land tenure have always been a part of such tenure and significantly vary. Furthermore, there is evidence of the judicial recognition of stronger individual tenure rights in different forms and in different states. Sweeping generalisations of the impact of privatisation across Africa should be approached with caution. African states differ, as this chapter has shown, and so does the impact of statutory and constitutional reform processes. Whether privatisation has impacted indigenous law is thus a contextual question and requires tact.

Second, if privatisation is as old as Africa, it is easy to imagine that different shades of this enterprise will continue. The periodisation of indigenous land tenure reform sketched in chapter "An Overview of Indigenous Land Tenure in Africa" provides a useful context to understand that tenure reform is an ongoing process shaped by different forces and requires caution in generalisations. For example, the binary tension that is often promoted about indigenous African land tenure being either individual or communal may miss the point about the intricate interwovenness of both and that one cannot exist without the other. Indigenous African law promotes both interests in different communities with varying success. Reform processes often seek to adjust and blunt anachronistic principles and tendencies of indigenous law that find expression in tenurial principles. For example, the recent promotion and establishment of gender access to indigenous land tenure is considered in more detail in chapter "Patriarchy, Gender, and Access to Indigenous Land Tenure in Africa" of this book and reflects a resounding rejection of patriarchy, which is a socially constructed principle that blights indigenous land tenure. The point cannot be made enough that gender equality has fundamentally improved indigenous land tenure. As noted in chapter "The Privatisation of Indigenous Land Tenure Development and the Future of African Indigenous Law", the organic development of indigenous land tenure to address gender access was slow to come, providing a justification for constitutional and legislative intervention.

Third, a useful standard of an assessment of the impact of indigenous land tenure reform is its impact on the ownership and management of communities. If land is a critical mass in the way indigenous communities address their political, economic, social, and spiritual concerns, the way communal management is conceived in several African states is important. Again, improved gender access and representation, as mentioned above, are crucial. Other mechanisms of communal management of indigenous land tenure are explored in the following and reflect some of the internal tensions in indigenous communities that often accompany reform processes. Members of indigenous communities reflect their individual interests in their continuous struggle for participation in tenurial management at a family and community level. These internal struggles are often forgotten if change is attributed only to constitutional and statutory reform. To the extent that these struggles are recognised in one form or another, indigenous law is enhanced because these 'new' or 'improved' forms of communal management become part of the norms of an indigenous community.

Fourth, a feature of the privatisation of indigenous land tenure in several states is the control handed to communities and families to sanction such privatisation. Although alienation to a third party is the preferred form of privatisation, the conversion process in Uganda stands out because it is easy to imagine that states such as Uganda, where there is a conversion process from customary land to statutory land, doom the tenure of communal indigenous land. There is no doubt that conversion speed up the process of the disestablishment of indigenous land tenure, which is not inevitable. This is not necessarily true because there is an implicit understanding that indigenous communal land tenure should continue, since conversion is not automatic, but with the consent of members of the family and tenure authorities. Even in states that do not expressly recognise conversion, tenure law and practices in countries like Nigeria allow such conversion through registration of instruments of transfer of indigenous land into individual land holdings. The recognition of indigenous land tenure as a form of land holding in Nigeria creates considerable tensions and often shifts the burden to indigenous families and communities to strategically protect their communal land tenure. Family consent to alienating indigenous land tenure in Nigeria and Uganda is reflective of a balance between the preservation of indigenous land tenure and socio-economic pressures. This is also the balance that appears to motivate the recognition of leaseholds in Namibia. Namibia is unique for the fact that the freehold title cannot be part of the indigenous land tenure except in the form of leaseholds. Sierra Leone is another example of family and community-mediated privatisation of indigenous land tenure, especially in light of a history of inferior recognition of indigenous law in many African states. Statutory recognition of mechanisms that enhance indigenous law overcomes recognition rules such as the repugnancy clauses that are arbitrary and discretionary in the determination of what is just and in good conscience.

Fifth, another feature of the privatisation of indigenous land tenure is the introduction of broad-based indigenous land management that is largely insulated from traditional authorities. This immunisation includes statutory authorities that alienate indigenous land tenure, such as Botswana Land Boards and Nigeria's Land Use Allocation Committees. Other mechanisms include statutory bodies that are empowered to confirm alienation and allocation of indigenous land tenure, such as Tanzania's Village Assembly, Namibia's Land Boards, and Uganda's Land Board. In a country like Ghana, where traditional authorities retain their traditional tenurial powers, new mechanisms such as the Customary Land Secretariats have been established and appear to have had some impact on the democratisation and functionality of some forms of indigenous land administration. The importance of a broad-based indigenous land management is found in paragraph 17 of the 2017 Kenyan Community Land Regulations, which recognises the ability of a community to convert its land to private land. Such an orderly process recognises the pressure of privatisation within the framework of a communal indigenous land tenure paradigm. The Kenyan conversion process ensures that incidents of indigenous land tenure can be grafted into tenurial transition and ensure that the principles of indigenous land tenure can be preserved.

Sixth, communal ownership and management are improved when the reform process recognises the autonomy of indigenous communities to develop aspects of their norms, enabling them to encode customary practices, norms, rules, processes, and institutions in the privatisation process. Since indigenous communities do not author reform legislation, some features of this model stray from indigenous law and, in practice, are completely ignored or altered by indigenous communities. Some of the interesting dimensions of the models of privatisation that recognise individual interests recognise community development of management protocols around broad guidelines. These protocols represent the development and codification of indigenous law around which indigenous communities are encouraged to debate their normative development. This fact recognises the 'constant' flux of developmental needs of indigenous communities and the need for a broad-based consensus. Whether these have been successful is a matter of conjecture, even though it is clear that this model is the preferred way of protecting indigenous land tenure that contemplates individual interests if the recent reform processes in Ghana, Kenya, Sierra Leone, and Liberia are a yardstick of measure. Indigenous law will survive and thrive where internal norm-making is recognised and protected. Written protocols of indigenous tenure management negate the widespread belief that orality is a fundamental aspect of indigenous law. These protocols encourage indigenous communities to adopt broad guidelines. It is true that writing would affect the inherent flexibility of indigenous law and blunt its capacity to respond to changes in many respects. However, if truth be told, orality has blighted the development of indigenous law and entrenched its inferior status. There is always the possibility that it may be hijacked by individuals and traditional authorities who offer self-serving interpretations.

Seventh, an issue that is not well considered is whether secondary rights and other responsibilities of indigenous land tenure follow a private interest. Another way of conceiving this issue is whether members of such communities can ignore the social functions of indigenous land tenure that arise from the membership of such a group. For example, would a concept of individual indigenous land tenure that contemplates many interests over the same piece of land promote the principles of indigenous land tenure and be a worthy objective to pursue? Would it be possible, for example, for access to a private interest to be granted to other members of a community, even to foreigners, to allow them to graze their animals or pursue other social ends in the traditional and socially compliant indigenous land tenure framework? Another way to approach the issue is to ask whether there is evidence that certain incidents of indigenous law follow privatised land? The example of Articles 32 and 38 of Ethiopia's 2024 Land Proclamation demands more attention as a means to ensure that some incidents of indigenous land tenure law interests follow privatised land. In addition, the land use restrictions imposed by Article 32 on rural land, which contemplates private land until a Land Use Plan is approved, seem worthy of emulation and reflect the communal context of privatised land. Article 38 approves the possibility of leasing pastoral land with the consent of three-quarters of the community, but burdens the lease with access to the grazing land.

Eighth, it is inevitable to compare the two models of privatisation, and it appears that support for the model that expressly recognises privatisation within a family and communal context is preferable. This model leans heavily on the norms of indigenous law that the formalisation process has replicated or revised. Furthermore, the principles of indigenous law are likely crucial in elaborating on this model. Of far more importance is the fact that the community-centric model would lead to a revitalisation of the indigenous communities of Africa, enabling them to play a more crucial role in the governance of Africa. The other model of state ownership of indigenous land tenure can also protect indigenous land tenure if appropriate care is taken in some measure of communal control, as evidenced by the Tanzanian system. Both models can be of considerable assistance if the goal of restoring Africa's indigenous communities through a redesign of their indigenous land tenure is a goal of the reform process, but one that is inevitable. One reason for this state of affairs is that, since post-colonial Africa has struggled to find relevance for indigenous communities, it is important to think carefully about reform within the context of promoting and preserving the material culture of indigenous communities in general and their preferred tenure understandings.[209]

5 Conclusion

Since there is a long history and evidence of the co-existence of individual and communal land tenure in indigenous communities, it appears reasonable to imagine that increasingly African states recognise the fact that communities can privatise their land tenure within their norms, values, and institutions.[210] If it so decides, a process that will continue as communities respond to external stimuli and strive to survive all manner of crises. Janet Banda notes this point:

> More importantly, the concept of individual ownership under customary tenure should be recognized so as to pursue reforms that are consistent with this concept to preserve the objectives of customary tenure, which support individual rights concurrent with communal interests and promote food, social security, and dynamism.[211]

A community-led privatisation programme ensures a favourable future for indigenous law. However, the consequences of Africa's plural legal orders are that the reform process often mimics state land tenurial arrangements, especially in circumstances of exasperation with the failings of indigenous land tenure. This feeling is evident in several commentators who advocate the merger of both systems built on state tenurial systems.[212] The implications of this viewpoint would be the disappearance of the indigenous land tenure and the indigenous law.

---

[209] It should be pointed out that some of the reform processes of indigenous land tenure in several African countries point to a need to develop indigenous land tenure within the context of indigenous law. For example, The Rukuni Commission of Inquiry into Appropriate Agricultural Land Tenure Systems in Zimbabwe *Report of the Commission of Inquiry into Appropriate Agricultural Land Tenure Systems* (1994) that stated that: 'the current legislation on communal land rights for the communities and households [should] be amended to strengthen the security of tenure. Statutory laws have to be cognisant of customary law on land which is still widely practised and any new or consolidated laws have to encode at least the common principles of customary law and the spirit behind the law. Customary law and procedures have to be continually understood, written down and formalised as by-laws in various Rural Districts.'

[210] Alden Wiley (2008), pp. 43–52; Alden Wiley (2011a), pp. 733–757; Alden Wiley (2011b) Alden Wiley (2012).

[211] See Banda (2011), pp. 312–355, 334.

[212] See, for example, Blocher (2006), p. 177; Arko-Adjei (2011).

References

Abdo M (2014) State policy and law in relation to land alienation in Ethiopia. Dissertation, University of Warwick, p 204

Abdullahi M (2007) The legal status of the communal land holding system in Ethiopia: the case of pastoral communities. Int J Minor Group Rights:85–125

Adams M (2003) Land tenure policy and practice in Botswana: governance lessons for southern Africa. Available at https://mokoro.co.uk/wp-content/uploads/land_tenure_policy__practice_botswana.pdf. Accessed 13 Oct 2025

Agbosu L, Awumbilla M, Dowuona-Hammond C, Tsikata D (2007) Customary and statutory land tenure and land policy in Ghana. ISSER Technical Publication No. 70

Agegnehu SK, Mansberger R (2020) Community involvement and compensation money utilization in Ethiopia: case studies from Bahir Dar and Debre Markos Peri Urban Areas. Sustain 12:4794. https://doi.org/10.3390/su12114794

Akwensivie G, Abedi-Lartey AM (2021) Appraisal of thirty-three customary land secretariats in Ghana. Afr J Land Policy Geospatial Sci 5(3):553–570

Alden Wiley L (2008) Custom and commonage in Africa rethinking the orthodoxies. Land Use Policy 25:43–52

Alden Wiley L (2011a) The law is to blame: the vulnerable status of common property rights in sub-Saharan Africa. Dev Change 42(3):733–757

Alden Wiley L (2011b) Customary land tenure in the modern world, rights to resources in crisis: reviewing the fate of customary tenure in Africa, Brief No 1. Rights and Resources Initiative, Washington DC

Alden Wiley L (2012) Land reform in Africa: a reappraisal. reviewing the fate of customary tenure in Africa, Brief No 3, Rights and Resources Initiative, Washington DC

Alden Wiley L (2018) The Community Land Act in Kenya opportunities and challenges for communities. Land 7(1):12. https://doi.org/10.3390/land7010012

Amnesty International (2019) Angola: land, basic rights and freedoms. https://www.amnesty.org/en/wp-content/uploads/2021/05/AFR1201852019ENGLISH.pdf. Accessed 13 October 2025

Arko-Adjei A (2011) Adapting land administration to the institutional framework of customary tenure: the case of peri-urban Ghana. IOS Press, Ghana

Asaaga F, Hirons MA (2019) Windows of opportunity or windows of exclusion? Changing dynamics of tenurial relations in rural Ghana Land Use Policy 87. https://doi.org/10.1016/j.landusepol.2019.104042

Banda J (2011) Romancing customary tenure challenges and prospects for the neo-liberal suitor. In: Fenrich J, Galizzi P, Higgins T (eds) The future of African customary law. Cambridge University Press, pp 312–355, 334

Bentsi-Enchill K (1964) Ghana land law: an exposition and critique. Sweet & Maxwell, London

Blocher J (2006) Building on custom: land tenure policy and economic development in Ghana. Yale Human Rights Dev Law J 9:177

Budy FCT (2018) Neo-colonialism, Land Grabbing and the Land Rights Act, 2014 Liberia Studies. Program 43:189–216

Chenitz ZS, Richardson A (2013) Taking stock of the risks associated with the individualization of land rights. In: Mostert H, Verstappen L, Zevenbergen J, Van Schalkwyk L (eds) Land law and governance: African perspectives on land tenure and title. Juta, Cape Town, p 113

Chigbu U, Alemayehu Z, Dachaga W (2019) Uncovering land tenure insecurities: tips for tenure responsive land-use planning in Ethiopia. Dev Pract 29:371–383. https://doi.org/10.1080/09614524.2019.1567688

Chimhowu A, Woodhouse P (2006) Customary vs private property rights? dynamics and trajectories of vernacular land markets in sub-saharan Africa. J Agrarian Change 346

Christopher AJ (1995) Land Restitution in South Africa, 1991–1994. Land Use Policy 12:267–279

Claassens A, Ngubane S (2008) Women, land and power: the impact of the Communal Land Rights Act. In: Claassens A, Cousins B (eds) Land, power and custom: controversies generated by South Africa's Communal Land Rights Act. Legal Resources Centre, p 154

Cousins B (2013) Women's land rights and social change in rural South Africa: the Case of Msinga, KwaZulu-Natal. In: Claassens A, Smythe D (eds) Marriage, law & custom: what's law got to do with it? Juta, Cape Town, pp 73–99

De Quadros MC (n.d.) Current land policy issues in Mozambique. https://www.fao.org/4/y5026e/y5026e0c.htm. Accessed 10 July 2023

De Sousa Santos B (2006) The heterogeneous state and legal pluralism in Mozambique. Law Soc Rev 40:59–75

Delius P, Beinart W (2021) Securing the land: from customary land tenure to registered titled land? In: Mbasa K, Mbasa B (eds) Land in South Africa: contested meanings and nation building. Mistra, Johannesburg, pp 84–109

Di Matteo F (2021). The emergence of "Community Land" in Kenya: Land Tenure Reforms in National Policy Processes and Community Mobilizations. Research series. Paris, French Technical Committee on Land Tenure and Development (AFD-MEAE)

Dieterle C (n.d.) Global governance meets local land tenure: international codes of conduct for responsible land investments in Uganda. J Dev Stud 58:582–589

Du Plessis E, Frantz G (2013) African customary land rights in a private ownership paradigm. SSRN: https://ssrn.com/abstract=2381922 or https://doi.org/10.2139/ssrn.2381922. Accessed 4 Apr 2024

Du Plessis W, Pienaar J (2010) The more things change, the more they stay the same: the story of communal land tenure in South Africa. Fundamina 16:73–89

Feinberg HM (2009) Black South African initiatives and the land, 1913-1948. J Contemp Hist 34(2):39–61

Gebreamanuel DH (2011) Land use legislation in Ethiopia: A human rights and environment based analysis. Jimma Univ J Law:1–31

Ghebru H, Pitoro R, Woldeyohannes S (2015) Customary tenure and innovative measures of safeguarding land rights in Africa: The Community Land Initiative (Iniciativa de Terras Comunitárias) in Mozambique. IFPRI Discussion Paper 01484

Hall R (2004) Land Restitution in South Africa: Rights, Development, and the Restrained State. Canadian J Afr Stud Revue Canadienne Des Études Africaines 38:654–671. https://doi.org/10.1080/00083968.2004.10751302

Hull S, Whittall J (2018) Filling the gap: customary land tenure reform in Mozambique and South Africa. South Afr J Geomat Afr GEO Special Edition 7:2–117

Iwarere LJ (2008) Property rights and land market dynamics: an economic interpretation of the indigenous land tenure transformation process in Nigeria. In: Simons RA, Malmgren R, Small G (eds) Indigenous peoples and real estate valuation. research issues in real estate, vol 10. Springer, Boston, pp 201–227. https://doi.org/10.1007/978-0-387-77938-6_10

Kasanga K, Kotey NA (2001) Land management in Ghana: building on tradition and modernity. IIED, London

Kingwill R (2017) An inconvenient truth: Land title in social context – a South African perspective. In: Mostert H, Verstappen L, Zevenbergen J, Van Schalkwyk L (eds) Land law and governance: African perspectives on land tenure and title. Juta, Cape Town, p 65

Kludze AKP (1987) Accountability of the head of family in Ghana: a statutory solution in search of a problem. J Afr Law 31:107–118

Lambrecht I, Asare S (2016) The complexity of local tenure systems: A smallholders perspective on tenure in Ghana. Land Use Policy 58:251–263

Liberia-The World Factbook. https://www.cia.gov/the-world-factbook/countries/liberia/

Maila S, Raboshakga N, Nwauche ES, Du Plessis W (2023) Communal land tenure: Past, present and future – Accommodating division and allocation of land in the context of development with reference to the Limpopo Province in South Africa and other African jurisdictions. In: Horn JG, Pienaar JM, Wiese M (eds) Protean scholar: essays in honour of professor Gerrit Pienaar. Juta, Cape Town, pp 41–42

Mailula D (2011) Customary (communal) land tenure in South Africa: did Tongoane overlook or avoid the core issue? Const Court Rev 4:73–112

Mandondo A (2000) Situating Zimbabwe's Natural Resource Governance Systems in History CIFOR Occasional Paper 32. Available at https://www.cifor-icraf.org/publications/pdf_files/OccPapers/OP-32.pdf. Accessed 1 Nov 2025

Morolong S, Ng'ong'ola C (2007) Revisiting the notion of ownership of tribal land in Botswana. In: Fombad CM (ed) Essays on law in Botswana. Juta, Cape Town, pp 142–175

Mostert H (2010) South Africa's communal land rights act: a plea for restraint in reform. J Afr Law 54(2):298–312. https://doi.org/10.1017/S0021855310000094

Ncube GT (2011) Crisis of communal leadership: Post-colonial local government reform and administrative conflict with traditional authorities in the communal areas of Zimbabwe, 1980-2008. Afr J Hist Cult 89

Ng'ong'ola C (1992) Land problems in some peri-urban villages in Botswana, and problems of conception, description and transformation of 'tribal' land tenure. J Afr Law 36:140–167

Ng'ong'ola C (1996) Land tenure reform in Botswana: post-colonial developments and future prospects. South Afr Pub Law 11:1–29

Ng'ong'ola C (1997) Land rights for marginalised ethnic groups in Botswana, with special reference to Basarwa. J Afr Law 41:1–26

Ng'ong'ola C (2017) Reflections on Botswana's 2015 land policy. Univ Botswana Land Policy 24:113–139

Ng'ong'ola C (2019) Botswana's Tribal Land Act of 2018: confounding innovations with congenital and other defects. Univ Botswana Law J, pp 3–35

Odote C, Rahma H, Husna M (2021) Over promising while under-delivering: implementation of Kenya's Community Land Act. Afr J Land Policy Geospatial Sci 4(2):291–307

Ollennu NA (1985) Principles of customary land law in Ghana, 2nd edn. Sweet & Maxwell, London

Orani M, Schemers J (2017) The recognition of the customary land rights: lessons from the Province of Bié in Angola. https://landportal.org/library/resources/recognition-customary-land-rights-lessons-province-bie-angola. Accessed 13 Oct 2025

Oshio PE (1989) Mortgages under the rights of occupancy system in Nigeria. J Afr Law 33(1):19–30. https://doi.org/10.1017/S0021855300007956

Oxford Learner's Dictionaries. https://www.oxfordlearnersdictionaries.com/definition/american_english/administer. Accessed 27 Feb 2022

Roux T (2006) Land restitution and reconciliation in South Africa. In: Du Bois F, du Bois—Pedain A (eds) Justice and Reconciliation in Post--Apartheid South Africa 144–171

Ryan C (2024) Invoking 'the Customary' in the Formalization of Land Reform in Liberia and Sierra Leone. J Interv Statebuild 19:66–87. https://doi.org/10.1080/17502977.2024.2385037

Unruh J (2008) Land policy reform, customary rule of law and the peace process in Sierra Leone. Afr J Leg Stud 2:94–117

Van den Brink R (2008) Land reform in Mozambique. Agric Rural Dev Notes 43:1–4

Van der Walt (1995) Land reform in South Africa since 1990 – an overview. SAPL 10:1–30

Weinberg T (2021) A history of communal property associations in South Africa. In: Beinart W, Kingwill R, Capps G (eds) Land, law and chiefs in rural South Africa: contested histories and current struggles. Wits University Press, pp 208–228

Werner W (2021) Land governance on communal land in Namibia land, environment and development project. Land, Environment and Development Project Legal Assistance Centre, pp 1–44

Wilson, PJ, Du Plessis PG, Pienaar J (2000) Land claims of indigenous peoples—the impact on property values: a comparative study on South Africa and Australia. J Real Estate Liter 8:35–56

Woodman G (1996) Customary land law in the Ghanaian courts. Ghana Universities Press, Ghana

Patriarchy, Gender, and Access to Indigenous Land Tenure in Africa

Contents

1 Introduction 87
2 Constitutional Frameworks for Gender Equality 90
3 Statutory Recognition of Women's Access to Indigenous Land Tenure 92
4 Conclusion 96
References 97

1 Introduction

This chapter highlights what may be considered a significant contribution of the reform of indigenous land tenure in Africa to sustainable indigenous land tenure in Africa. The provision for gender equality in indigenous land tenure is universal in African states and bodes well for the future of indigenous land tenure because it reverses centuries of gender inequality in indigenous governance that followed in the wake of colonialism and Africa's post-colonial states. Gender inequality is socially constructed in indigenous communities in Africa[1] and should not have become a signpost for these communities. It is often orthodox that patriarchy and gender inequality are fundamental to indigenous communities. If it is socially constructed, it means in principle that these communities could change their norms to recognise gender equality.

Decades of waiting for the organic development of these communities towards the recognition of gender equality have been frustrating. Radical judicial engagement towards equality based on constitutional and statutory provisions of indigenous laws in Africa reinforces the basic humanity of indigenous communities. Although the goal of gender inequality remains elusive, as this chapter reveals, statutory recognition of equal access to indigenous land tenure secures a great future for indigenous land tenure in Africa.

[1] See, for example, Chanock (1985).

E. Nwauche, *The Privatisation of Indigenous Land Tenure and the Future of African Indigenous Law*, https://doi.org/10.1007/978-3-032-14881-0_4

That the legislative and judicial enhancement of women's access to indigenous land tenure as a significant and positive feature of the privatisation of indigenous land tenure in Africa is remarkable. The widespread concern for patriarchy and gender discrimination in access to succession and inheritance of property in African countries ensured that the legislative reform of indigenous land tenure was anchored on the need to ensure that women accessed, owned, and inherited indigenous land tenure as articulated by national legal systems.

The fact that women, who make up almost half of the African population, perform maternal functions and take the lead in African rural economies, suggests that ignoring their access and participation in the management of indigenous land tenure would strip Africa of the gravitas to mobilise the indigenous land tenure for the development of communities and their states. As South Africa's Presidential Advisory Panel on Land Matters remarked:

> Rights to control and use land are central to the lives of rural women, whose lives and livelihoods are derived from the land and its natural resources. The lack of land rights for women and girls threatens their living conditions, their economic empowerment, their physical well-being and their struggle for equality within a patriarchal society … Rules of access and inheritance in rural societies favour men over women and women with children over those without.[2]

Waves of constitutional design incorporating gender equality and outlawing discrimination did not bridge the gap between constitutional text and social practice, denying women a place and a significant voice at the indigenous land tenure table. Women are less likely to have access to control and manage indigenous land tenure in many parts of Africa without guaranteed places in indigenous land management institutions.

This chapter addresses how several African countries have used the reform of communal indigenous tenure to ensure women's access to such tenure and abolish, curtail, and motivate patriarchal features in their country and argues that the reform of communal indigenous land tenure coupled with the judicial recognition of gender equality in several African states has had an appreciable impact on women's access to indigenous land tenure and community development. Consequently, as the chapter reveals, several states have reformed indigenous land tenure with partial success. If law reform were the only measure, women's access to land would have been secured decades ago. Of course, there is often a wide gulf between social norms, practices, and understandings that do not adhere to statutory law, with the consequences that women have inadequate access to ownership and management of indigenous land tenure in Africa.[3]

A fundamental challenge of indigenous land tenure is the extent to which women are recognised as equal to men in relation to their capacity to inherit land; ownership of individual land within a communal land tenure; headship of families and recipients of land transferred in the subdivision of communal and family land. In a

[2] See Presidential Advisory Panel on Land Reform and Agriculture (2019), pp. 36–37.

[3] See, for example, Whitehead and Tsikata (2003), pp. 67–112; Ossome (2014), pp. 155–177.

continent where patriarchy is touted as one of the defining features of indigenous law, an inquiry into the privatisation of indigenous land tenure must examine whether all genders can have access to indigenous land and enjoy the benefits of privatisation as important as whether privatisation can thrive within or destroy communal land tenure. If women were wrongly excluded from the tenure of indigenous land to the detriment of Africa, the project of privatisation of indigenous land tenure would be severely challenged.

This chapter also addresses the participation of women in indigenous land tenure in two distinct ways out of the three possible ways women acquire land in Africa, that is, by inheriting land and the subdivision of indigenous communal land. We are not so concerned with interests in land that women acquire themselves or with their spouses. Our concern with succession rights follows the previous chapter, where the capacity of indigenous women to be allocated land is a feature of the legislative development of communal land tenure in several African states. Without concomitant succession rules, these legislative victories for women mean very little. Consequently, except where such legislative recognition of gender equality changes customary law rules of inheritance, customary rules of inheritance that survive legislative developments are crucial in women's access to indigenous land tenure.[4]

If patriarchy is one of the fundamental features of indigenous law in Africa, evaluating the prospect of gender equality through statutory and judicial reform is vital to assessing the future of indigenous law in Africa. A strong belief that our indigenous norms are socially constructed and that each epoch is a product of unique political and socio-economic circumstances motivates this chapter. There is nothing inevitable about indigenous norms, nor are they immemorial and immutable. Patriarchy developed within a particular socioeconomic period of African history. But Africa is in a period of liberal constitutionalism and rights, where rapid advances enable us to question why more than half of Africans are discriminated against on the grounds of gender. Change occurs from within and without, with the latter often as drastic and transformative as the former. The idea of privatising Indigenous land tenure and equal rights for Indigenous men and women is epochal. It can be stated that indigenous law is greatly enriched.

This chapter addresses the statutory alteration of patriarchal features of indigenous law in Africa as a standard feature of the legislative development of indigenous land tenure. Without fail, recent land tenure legislation recognises the equality of women to hold and be allocated indigenous land upon the subdivision of communal or family land. Such provisions reinforce constitutional commitments to quality and non-discrimination based on sex and gender. In addition, women are included in the management of communal land tenure.

[4] See, for example, McAuslan (2013), p. 221.

2 Constitutional Frameworks for Gender Equality

Several African constitutions adopt different mechanisms to promote gender equality. First, through the recognition of various rights such as dignity, life, equality, and non-discrimination based on gender. The second is through the prohibition of harmful cultural practices against women, and the third is through affirmative action. African judiciaries, in their interpretation of these gender-affirming provisions, have struck down different patriarchal and discriminatory indigenous law principles and practices. One aspect of the access of women and girls was their inability to succeed in their fathers' and husbands' land, as well as to have family headship. Succession in the context of indigenous law must therefore be understood to refer to the process of succeeding to the status of the deceased person. The perpetuation and preservation of the family unit and succession to the position and status of the deceased, therefore, lie at the heart of succession in indigenous law. The purpose of indigenous law of succession is, therefore, to protect the family and ensure that the dependents of the deceased are looked after. This is achieved by entrusting the responsibility of looking after the welfare of the deceased's dependants to one person in return for the right to control family property. This system ensures that the dependants of the deceased, as well as members of the family, always have a home and resources towards for their maintenance. This prevents homelessness. Those who cannot support themselves, such as minor children, have someone to support and maintain them.

As argued above, removing the discrimination against women would ensure that they can become the head of a family entrusted with the administration and protection of family property. For example, the Nigerian judiciary bins a series of cases, including *Muojekwu v Muojekw*u;[5] *Ejikeme v Muojekwu*;[6] *Muojekwu* v *Iwuchukwu*[7]; *Nnayelugo v Nnayelugo*[8] ; and *Asika v Atuanya.*[9] Nigerian courts of Appeal have used Section 42 of the 1999 Constitution of the Federal Republic of Nigeria and other constitutional provisions to affirm the rights of Nigerian daughters and wives to inherit the properties of their fathers and husbands.[10]

In the celebrated South African case of *Bhe v Magistrate Khayelitsha*,[11] the principle of primogeniture was struck down and the rights of wives and daughters to succeed in land tenure were recognised, meaning that in the context of indigenous land tenure, daughters and wives can succeed to individual land held by a husband

[5] [1997] 7 NWLR (Pt 512) 283.

[6] [2000] 5 NWLR (Pt 657) 418.

[7] [2004] ALL FWLR (Pt 211) 1406.

[8] [2008] All FWLR Pt 401 897.

[9] 2008 All FWLR (Pt. 433) 1293.

[10] A representative literature of the salience of constitutional affirmation of gender equality in Nigeria includes Diala (2018a), pp. 155–174. Diala (2018b), pp. 706–731; Ewelukwa (2002), pp. 427–428; Iwobi (2008), pp. 37–86.

[11] 2005 (1) SA 580.

or father. The degree of recognition of inheritance rights in South Africa does not address the issues of access to indigenous land tenure that is controlled by traditional authorities and formed part of the motivation for the enactment of the ill-fated Communal Land Rights Act of 2004.

In Tanzania, discrimination on the grounds of sex is explicitly prohibited by Articles 12 and 13 of the Constitution,[12] leading to litigation seeking to strike down discriminatory inheritance rules of customary law. In a number of cases, such as *Edward v Neckemia,*[13] *Rugimbana v Rugimbana*,[14] and *Kamugisha v Kamugisha*,[15] Tanzanian courts have held that customary law, which prohibits women from inheriting land, violated the Tanzanian Constitution. Even though there have been setbacks in the constitutional recognition of gender equality in some African states,[16] an overwhelming majority of African states constitutionally recognise gender equality.[17] Women's access to land tenure has also been facilitated by treaties such as the Convention on the Elimination of All Forms of Discrimination against Women (CEDAW); the African Charter on Human and Peoples' Rights; and Protocol to the African Charter on Human and Peoples' Rights on the Rights of Women in Africa (the Maputo Protocol). For example, paragraph 2 of the Maputo Protocol provides that:

> Women shall enjoy, on the basis of equality with men, the same rights and respect for their dignity and contribute to the preservation of those African cultural values that are positive and are based on the principles of equality, dignity, justice and democracy.

There is little doubt that women's statutory and constitutional access to indigenous land tenure is in support of the Maputo Protocol.[18]

---

[12] Articles 12 and 13 of the Constitution of the United Republic of Tanzania provide as follows: '12. (1) All human beings are born free and are equal. (2) Every person is entitled to recognition and respect for his dignity. 13.(1) All persons are equal before the law and are entitled, without any discrimination, to protection and equality before the law. (2) No law enacted by any authority in the United Republic shall make any provision that is discriminatory either of itself or in its effect. (3) The civic rights, duties and interests of every person and community shall be protected and determined by the courts of law or other state agencies established by or under the law. (4) No person shall be discriminated against by any person or any authority acting under any law or in the discharge of the functions or business of any state office.'

[13] [2020] TZHC 4264.

[14] [2020] TZHC 4394.

[15] [2020] TZHC 954.

[16] Note the use of claw-back principles in the Zimbabwe Constitution, which has been problematic for gender equality. See, for example, *Magaya v Magaya* SC No. 210-98.

[17] See further, Art 27(4)d of the Constitution of Sierra Leone 1991; sect 33 of the 1995 Uganda Constitution; and Arts 27 and 40 of the Kenyan Constitution.

[18] Geng (2019); Mutambasere et al. (2023).

3 Statutory Recognition of Women's Access to Indigenous Land Tenure

A prominent feature of the statutory reform of indigenous land tenure the focus on and recognition of women's access to indigenous land tenure. To address women's marginalisation, several African states through legislation[19] have directly and indirectly recognised women as equal to men as they legislate in different forms—as shown in the previous chapter—the privatisation of interests in communal indigenous land tenure. Three mechanisms are evident. The first is through a statutory affirmation of the right of women to hold private interests in indigenous land tenure. The second is by requiring minimum quotas for women representation in land tenure management institutions that are charged with determining the boundaries of, and interest in, indigenous land; adjudicating upon and deciding issues of customary land tenure, as well as safeguarding the interests of women, absent persons, minors, and persons under a disability in the allocation and management of indigenous land tenure. The results of these interventions are limited, but are widely recognised as a veritable foundation around which more women are accessing communal land in several African countries.

Several land tenure reform legislations recognise and, in some cases, prioritise women's entitlement to access and enjoy indigenous land tenure. For example, Ethiopia's 2024 Rural Land Administration and Use Proclamation in Article 4 provides for affirmative action for women to access rural land. Another example is found in Article 39, which requires that income from communal land rent compensation, and sales of any produce be deposited in the Communal Land Users Fund, which is to provide support to economically disadvantaged women. Article 26 provides the last example of a requirement that irrigation and re-distribution of rural land shall consider the land rights of women. It should be noted that Article 5(1)c of the 2005 FDRE Rural Land Proclamation also recognised the right of women to use rural land. In Sierra Leone's Customary Land Rights Act of 2022, Section 5 is partly dedicated to gender equality. First, the right to own, hold, use, inherit, succeed, or deal with customary land is guaranteed to men and women equally. Second, any customary law that does not allow women to exercise the rights above is void. Third, the right to joint ownership of customary land where spouses acquire land. Fourth,

[19] Examples include Land Law 2004 of Angola; The Federal Land Use Proclamation of Ethiopia 2005; the Lesotho Land Act 2010; Communal Land Reform Act 2002 of Namibia; Zimbabwe's Communal Land Act 1982; Botswana's Tribal Land Act 1968; Zambia's Land Act 1995; Burkina Faso's Law No. 034-2009 on Rural Land Tenure; Côte d'Ivoire's Rural Land Law 1998; Kenya's Community Land Act 2018; Liberia's Land Rights Law 2018; Malawi's Customary Land Act 2016; Land Law of Mozambique 1997; Agricultural Land Law No 001 2017; South Sudan Land Act 2009; Uganda's 1998 Land Act; and the Republic of Congo's 2004 Law, Fixing Principles of General Application to National Land and Tenure as well as Law No.5 2011, Concerning Promotion and Protection of Rights of Indigenous Peoples; Tunisian 2016 Law of Collective Properties; and the Tanzanian Village Land Act 1999.

women are guaranteed headship and custodianship of family land and shall be entitled to share equally in the partition of family land.

Women's access to land is statutorily guaranteed in countries like Botswana, Nigeria, and Tanzania, where state ownership of land implies equal access. For example, in Tanzania, Section 3(2) of the Village Land Act protects the right of every adult woman to acquire, hold, use, deal with, and transmit by, or obtain land through the operation of a will, shall be to the same extent and subject to the same restrictions as the right of any adult man. Furthermore, any customs, traditions, and practices of the community may not be applied if they deny women lawful access to ownership, occupation, or use of land.

It is widely recognised that statutory-sanctioned gender equality provisions are often divorced from reality and ignore indigenous communities, providing a context to understand why the statutory reform of indigenous land tenure has, in addition, provided for the strategic positioning of women in indigenous land management bodies across Africa through mandated proportional female representation. In Sierra Leone, the CLRA 2022 reserves at least 30% of membership of land committees for women. Liberia is another African country that, through its 2018 Land Rights Act, mandates the establishment of a Community Land Development and Management Committee (CLDMC) through Article 36 to manage indigenous Liberian land. The membership of the CLDMC shall consist of equal representation of men, women, and youths. Even though the title is collectively held, the CLDMC is a body of the community charged with the governance and management of community land. Uganda's Land Act of 1998 (as amended) guarantees minimum women's representation in land management institutions at all governance levels. At the national level, at least one woman must be a member of the Uganda Land Commission, while one-third of the members of the District Land Boards must be women. Land Committees of each parish must have one woman as part of the four-member committee. At the local level, communal land management associations must have at least one-third female membership. In Namibia, four women are required to be members of Namibia's Communal Land Boards that are charged with exercising control over the allocation and the cancellation of customary land rights by chiefs or traditional authorities; evaluating applications for a right of leasehold as well as establishing and maintaining a register and a system of registration for recording the allocation, transfer, and cancellation of customary land rights and rights of leasehold.

Although South Africa's proposed Communal Land Rights Act (CLRA), which was passed in 2004, was declared unconstitutional in 2010 due to procedural lapses,[20] the provisions of that law reflected the idea of mandatory proportional representation of women in indigenous land management institutions, such as land administration committees, in the absence of recognised traditional councils. One-third of recognised traditional councils and/or land administration committees must

[20] See the case of *Tongoane and Others v the Minister of Agriculture and Land Affairs and Others* [2010] ZACC 10.

consist of women elected for a five-year tenure.[21] Since these institutions were not established, patriarchal traditional institutions have continued their control and management of indigenous land tenure. There is no doubt that women's participation in traditional councils is constrained by gender roles, economic disability, and male dominance, which are some of the reasons for strident opposition to the CLRA before its judicial demise.[22] Unfortunately, South Africa has not been fortunate enough to know whether such gendered land administration committees required by the CLRA would have made any difference to women's access to land in South Africa, as it appears to have done in several other African countries. It should be noted that the 2019 Traditional and Khoi San Leadership Act, around which South African traditional councils are organised, also mandates a 30% representation of women[23] in their task of performing functions provided for in terms of the customary law. However, there is evidence that even without the CLRA, South African women have negotiated access to user rights to indigenous land tenure within their families and communities.[24] Their negotiation and struggle for better tenure rights have underscored calls for elected and more women (at least 50%) members of traditional councils in South Africa[25] and Tanzania.[26]

The third mechanism to ensure women's access to indigenous land tenure is to designate them to indigenous land adjudication bodies that are as important, if not more, than land management institutions. These adjudicatory bodies are often traditional councils or special institutions introduced by land reform legislation. A good example is Tanzania's Village Land Act of 1999, which provides for a village adjudication committee, of which at least two women must be part of. The adjudication committee is statutorily charged to (i) determine the boundaries of and interest in land which is the subject of village adjudication; (ii) set aside or make reservations of land or demarcate rights of way and other easements which it considers necessary for the more beneficial occupation of land; (iii) adjudicate upon and decide in accordance with customary law any question referred to it by any person with an interest in land which is the subject of a village adjudication; (iii) advise the village adjudication adviser or any person subordinate to him who is assisting in the village adjudication process upon any question of customary law as to which its guidance has been sought; (iv) safeguard the interests of women, absent persons, minors, and persons under a disability; (v) take account of any interest in land in respect of which, for any reason, no claim has been made.

Women are also entitled to a quota by Section 43(2) of Sierra Leone's National Land Commission Act of 2022 to a 30% quota for women in chiefdom land committees who are statutorily enabled to manage communal chiefdom lands; enforce

---

21 See sects 21–24 of the CLRA establishing land administration committees.

22 See, for example, Pienaar (2009), pp. 1–16; Du Plessis and Pienaar (2010) 16:73–89.

23 See sect 16(2)(b) of the Traditional and Khoi-San Leadership Act 2019.

24 Claassens and Ngubane (2008), pp. 154–182.

25 Ibid., p. 174.

26 Schreiber (2017), p. 23.

rules for sustainable use of forests, grazing lands, rivers and swamps; adjudicate land title disputes through a sub-committee provided for in Section 78 of the Act.

An assessment of the three mechanisms for ensuring women's access to indigenous land tenure suggests modest outcomes from a review of academic commentary. Clearly, women's membership of land management committees and land rights adjudication bodies is a better mechanism than law reform that simply recognises the equality of women in access to indigenous land tenure without institutional support.

An assessment of the impact of women's representation in indigenous land management and adjudicatory bodies suggests modest outcomes. A few examples will suffice. First, while Tanzania's novel inclusion of women in land governance is celebrated, there is evidence that, although quotas for village assemblies have been met, there is a lack of active participation by women[27] and cultural pushback.[28] In Liberia, there are similar sentiments of attenuated women's participation in community land development management committees.[29] An analysis of the impact of the CLDMC is instructive:

> The 2018 Land Rights Act (LRA) brought a powerful change to the way communities care for their land… Liberian CSOs were instrumental during the development of the Land Rights Policy (2012), contributed to the drafting of the Land Rights Act, and briefed legislators during the law-making process…Their efforts helped ensure that local voices were included in the reform process, with a focus on ensuring that communities could manage and benefit from their land…The democratically elected Community Land Development and Management Committees (CLDMCs), made up of an equal number of men and women chosen by their neighbours, stepped up to meet the opportunity to control their destinies.[30]

Sierra Leone's experience of women's participation in the management of indigenous land tenure pursuant to the Customary Land Rights Act 2022 is also instructive according to Land for Life:

> Women make up a sizable proportion of the population of Sierra Leone, particularly in rural villages where land is used for agriculture and some economic benefits. Nonetheless, these women seldom own the land on which they are working or have tenure security or control over it. Women frequently have little decision-making ability and influence over how the land or its outputs are used. Previously, traditional authorities and other key players at the village and chiefdom levels determined the right to land for women in customary contexts … It is clear that the complete implementation of the Customary Land Rights Act will ensure women's rights to access land, resulting in more socioeconomic independence for them, particularly those in rural areas with restricted access to land.[31]

[27] See, for example, Massay (2016).

[28] Schreiber (2017), p. 18: The author recounts evidence during field work of '… both men and women were still under the impression that women weren't permitted to hold [occupancy certificates]'.

[29] See Tenure Facility (2025).

[30] See Tenure Facility (2025).

[31] See Land For Life (2023).

Although there are no statutory quotas for women's representation in Botswana's Communal Land Boards, Anne Griffiths' research[32] points to women's membership in the Kweneng Land Board; she studied and highlighted significant women's ownership of land certificates and leases.[33] Griffiths' research also points to different strategies Batswana women have used to access property. Economic empowerment, education and strategic positioning, and use of male powers are strategies African women have used to gain access to property, including indigenous land tenure. However, without fundamental legal changes, women's strategies to access property would struggle. Griffiths notes this point with respect to Botswana Communal Land Boards that were established to ensure that all citizens have equal access to all land that would ordinarily have been tribal land, under the control of traditional authorities[34] and difficult to access.

4 Conclusion

It remains a fact that women's involvement in the fora,[35] where customary law is made and interpreted, is crucial to the slow and steady change to customary practices, and the law is crucial to enforcing statutory and constitutional provisions of women's equality in accessing indigenous land tenure.

Africa's indigenous norms, principles, and law are socially constructed, and each epoch is a product of unique political and socio-economic circumstances. There is nothing inevitable about indigenous norms, nor are they immemorial and immutable. Patriarchy developed within a particular socioeconomic period of African history. In this era of liberal constitutionalism and rights, rapid advances such as the statutory reform of indigenous land tenure enable a pushback against gender inequality and inadequate access of African women to indigenous land tenure. Change occurs from within and without, with the latter often more drastic and transformative than the former. Legislation is a veritable means of social construction that challenges and responds to the slow and frustrating organic development of our indigenous laws. Africa is in an enormous developmental crisis, and it is easy to conclude that Africa does not have the luxury of waiting for organic development of gender equality in its indigenous societies.

[32] Griffiths (2011) 63:229–260.

[33] Ibid., p. 236.

[34] Ibid., pp. 239–240.

[35] See, for example, Ubink (2018).

References

Chanock M (1985) Law custom and social change: the colonial experience in Malawi and Zambia. Cambridge University Press, London

Claassens A, Ngubane S (2008) Women land and power: the impact of the Communal Land Rights Act. In: Claassens A, Cousins B (eds) Land power and custom: controversies generated by South Africa's Communal Land Rights Act. Legal Resources Centre, pp 154–182

Diala A (2018a) Legal pluralism and social change: insights from matrimonial property rights in Nigeria. In: Rautenbach C (ed) In the shade of an African Baobab: Tom Bennett's legacy. Juta, Cape Town, pp 155–174

Diala A (2018b) The shadow of legal pluralism in matrimonial property division outside the courts in southern Nigeria. Afr Human Rights Law J 18(2):706–731

Du Plessis W, Pienaar J (2010) The more things change, the more they remain the same: the story of communal land tenure in South Africa. Fundamina 16:73–89

Ewelukwa U (2002) Postcolonialism, gender, customary injustice: widows in African societies. Human Rights Quart 24(2):427–428

Geng J (2019) Chapter 24: The Maputo Protocol and the reconciliation of gender and culture in Africa. In: Research handbook on feminist engagement with international law. Edward Elgar Publishing, Cheltenham. https://doi.org/10.4337/9781785363924.00034

Griffiths A (2011) Delivering justice: the changing gendered dynamics of land tenure in Botswana. J Legal Pluralism 63:229–260

Iwobi AU (2008) No cause for merriment: the position of widows under Nigerian law. Canadian J Women Law 20:37–86

Land For Life (2023) Enhancing women's land rights in Sierra Leone: The intervention of Land for Life Initiative. Available at https://landforlife.org.sl/enhancing-womens-land-rights-in-sierra-leone-the-intervention-of-land-for-life-initiative/. 1 Nov 2025

Massay G (2016) Tanzania's Village Act 15 years on. Available at https://www.rural21.com 1st Nov 2025

McAuslan P (2013) Land law reform in Eastern Africa: traditional or transformative? Routledge, Abingdon, p 221

Mutambasere S, Budoo-Scholtz A, Murden D (eds) (2023) The impact of the Maputo Protocol in selected African states. PULP, Pretoria

Ossome L (2014) Can the law secure women's rights to land in Africa? Revisiting tensions between culture and land commercialization. Fem Econ 20:155–177

Pienaar G (2009) Regulating communal land rights: the story continues. Tydskrif vir Hedendaagse Romeins-Hollandse Reg 72:1–16

Presidential Advisory Panel on Land Reform and Agriculture (2019) Final Report of the Presidential Advisory Panel on Land Reform and Agriculture. Available at https://www.gov.za/sites/default/files/gcis_document/201907/panelreportlandreform_0.pdf 36–37) I Nov 2025

Schreiber L (2017) Registering Rural Rights: Village Land Titling in Tanzania, 2008–2017, p 23. Available at https://successfulsocieties.princeton.edu/sites/g/files/toruqf5601/files/LS_Tanzania_Land_GC.pdf 1 Nov 2025

Tenure Facility (2025) CLDMCs at the heart of Liberia's evolving land governance. Available at https://thetenurefacility.org/article/cldmcs-at-the-heart-of-liberias-evolving-land-governance/. 1 Nov 2025

Ubink J (2018) Customary legal empowerment in Namibia and Ghana? Lessons about access, power and participation in non-state justice systems. Dev Change 49:930–950. https://doi.org/10.1111/dech.12415

Whitehead A, Tsikata D (2003) Policy discourses on women's land rights in sub-Saharan Africa: the Implications of the re-turn to the customary. J Agrarian Change 3:67–112

References

[illegible]

Compulsory Acquisition of Indigenous Land Tenure in African States

Contents

1 Introduction 99
2 Indigenous Land Tenure and Elements of Compulsory Acquisition of Indigenous Lands in Africa 100
2.1 Legality 101
2.2 Determining 'Public Purpose' for Expropriating Indigenous Land 101
2.3 Procedure for Compulsory Acquisition 103
2.4 Payment of Compensation 107
2.5 Subsequent Use of Compulsorily Acquired Indigenous Land 110
3 Have African Judiciaries and Governments Failed Indigenous Peoples in the Large-Scale Acquisition of Indigenous Lands? 110
4 Conclusion 111
References 111

1 Introduction

This chapter returns to the idea that African states retain their capacity to excise and transform indigenous lands whether ownership and management of indigenous land tenure is recognised, and even more so, where the state holds the land. The size of indigenous land is important for communal management and ultimately privatisation. Where the size of indigenous land tenure is considerably reduced, the character, life, and worldview of the indigenous communities may be destroyed. Accordingly, although the state's power to appropriate indigenous land tenure may appear oblique to privatisation, the sanctity of indigenous land and when this may be breached demonstrates how the state imagines indigenous land tenure and is a proxy for privatisation. The argument can be put as follows. Why should the state not take over indigenous land where community and family members are entitled to own part of it? On the other hand, the rural nature of indigenous land predisposes it

E. Nwauche, *The Privatisation of Indigenous Land Tenure and the Future of African Indigenous Law*, https://doi.org/10.1007/978-3-032-14881-0_5

for acquisition for different public purposes.[1] It is, therefore, the nature of public purposes for which African states can expropriate indigenous land tenure that this chapter examines, including the question of whether the protection of indigenous land tenure is a public purpose.

While several instances of acquisition qualify as 'public purpose', the framework through which indigenous land tenure can be appropriated is as important as the question of whether members of indigenous communities have access to indigenous land tenure for various purposes, including alienation. The questionable exercise of compulsory acquisition is of grave concern because of the asymmetrical power relations between the state and indigenous communities. At the heart of compulsory acquisition is the search for a balance between two sides of the public interest: the objective of national development and the social, economic, and cultural lives of indigenous communities. As the case studies in this chapter indicate, the interests of indigenous communities are often overlooked for other development objectives of African states.

This chapter addresses long-standing frameworks of compulsory acquisition in African states from the perspective of indigenous land tenure and begins in the next section with a review of examples of compulsory acquisition of land, especially large-scale acquisition of indigenous land by foreign economic interests.

Inevitably, the size of indigenous land in Africa, often estimated to cover between 60% and 80% of Africa's land mass, and the asymmetrical relationship between indigenous communities and their states have led to questionable and challenging compulsory acquisition of indigenous land tenure. Case law and case studies across Africa suggest significant cases of compulsory acquisition.

Compulsory acquisition is an integral part of all governments, and the power of eminent domain enables the acquisition of land in the public interest. As such, a focus on indigenous land tenure may seem misplaced. To appreciate how compulsory acquisition of indigenous land tenure has fared in Africa, this chapter proceeds with an overview of the elements of compulsory acquisition and turns to a consideration of case law and case studies that highlight the experience and jurisprudence of several African courts and countries.

2 Indigenous Land Tenure and Elements of Compulsory Acquisition of Indigenous Lands in Africa

Generally, compulsory acquisition requires the elements of legality, public purpose, proper acquisition procedure, payment of equitable compensation, and judicial review. The recognition of the peculiar status of indigenous people has resulted in

---

[1] See, for example, Nyarko (2019), pp. 101, 100–125: 'Because land in Ghana is primarily owned by customary institutions and the state can only access land through the instrument of compulsory acquisition,17 the use of the government's power of compulsory acquisition is essential for several purposes.'

the requirement of adequate consultation and participation of indigenous communities. Indeed, some argue that the free, prior, and informed consent of indigenous peoples must be obtained for the compulsory acquisition of their land tenure.

2.1 *Legality*

Several African constitutions require that compulsory acquisition be legal or lawful, often referring to fidelity to expropriation legislation. For example, in Zambia, the procedure for the compulsory acquisition of land prescribed by the Lands Acquisition Act of 1995 is faithful to the spirit and intent of Article 16(1) of the Constitution.[2] The state must strictly follow the law and procedure for compulsory property acquisition as set out above. This is illustrated in the case of *Mpogwe Farms Limited (in Receivership) and Others v Attorney General*,[3] where the Court held that the Zambian state must follow the procedure set out in the Land Act in conformity with the rule of law.[4] Another example is in the Zimbabwean Constitution in Section 73(3)(a), which requires deprivation in terms of a law of general application. Even where there is no express legislative requirement or law specifically made for compulsory acquisition, most statutory schemes for compulsory acquisition of property in several African states satisfy the requirement of legality. For example, Ghana's State Lands Act 125 governs the acquisition of land in the national interest and the Administration of Lands Act 1962 (Act 123) grants the President the power to vest any customary land in himself/herself as trustee where it appears to the President that it is in the public interest to do so, which transforms the vesting into compulsory acquisition of indigenous tenure.

2.2 *Determining 'Public Purpose' for Expropriating Indigenous Land*

The constitutions of African states,[5] as well as land legislation,[6] provide for general public purposes and several specific ones. For example, in Ghana, Article 20 of the Constitution defines public purposes as the interest of defence, public safety, public

[2] See *Zambia National Holdings Limited and United National Independence Party (UNIP) v The Attorney-General* (1994) S.J. 22, 32 (S.C.).

[3] 2004/HP/0010.

[4] See also Lt General Musengule v Attorney General (2009) ZR 359.

[5] See for example Article 16 of the Zambian Constitution; section 25 of the 1996 Constitution of the Republic of South Africa; Article 17(4) of the Lesotho Constitution and section 26 of the Ugandan Constitution.

[6] See for example Nigerian Land Use Act (Chapter L4 Laws of Federal Republic of Nigeria); Ghana's Land Act 2020; Ethiopia's Expropriation of Landholdings for Public Purposes and

order, public morality, public health, town and country planning, or the development or utilisation of property in such a manner as to promote the public benefit. In Gambia, Article 22 of the Constitution provides that public purpose shall include the interest of defence, public safety, public order, public morality, public health, town and country planning, or the development or utilisation of any property in such a manner as to promote the public benefit; and (b) the necessity, therefore, is such as to afford reasonable justification of the causing of any hardship that may result to any person having any interest in or right over the property, and (c) provision is made by a law applicable to that taking of possession or acquisition.

Several African countries give the state absolute discretion in determining the purposes of compulsory acquisition. For example, Section 3 of Zambia's Land Act of 1995 endows the President of the country with absolute discretion whenever he thinks it is desirable or expedient in the interest of the Republic to do so, compulsorily acquire any property of any description. Even where such a wide discretion is not stated, the nature of the purposes imports such a wide discretion, especially when national courts are deferential to executive determinations.[7]

It is difficult for African courts to determine whether the expropriation of such lands to facilitate the privatisation of indigenous lands qualifies as a public purpose. It appears that the acquisition of indigenous land tenure enables the government to turn the land into state land, which can then be used for further governance, including redistributing the expropriated land to community members and other citizens. The Zimbabwean Constitutional Court alluded to this possibility in *Chikuta v Minister of Lands, Agriculture, Climate and Rural Settlement*.[8] Nigerian courts have opposed such reallocation of expropriated communal land to an individual. In *Awaogbo v Eze*,[9] a Nigerian court struck down the revocation of communal land to enable an apportionment of such land to community members.

Payment of Compensation Law 2005; Namibia's Communal Land Reform Act 2002 and South Sudan's 2009 Land Act.

[7] See, for example, sect 51 of Nigeria's Land Use Act lists the public purposes as '(a) for exclusive Government use or general public use; (b) for use by any statutory or government-controlled body corporate (c) for or in connection with sanitary improvements of any king; (d) for obtaining control over land contiguous to public transportation purposes; (f) for mining purposes; (g) for planned urban or rural development or settlement; (h) for economic, industrial or agricultural development.' See the following cases *Rossette Manufacturing v Ilemobola* [2007] 14 NWLR 109; *CSS Bookshop v RTMCRS* [2006] 11 NWLR 531.

[8] The Court stated that: 'A perusal of s 6 (3) of the Communal Land Act puts paid to the contention by the appellants that, as a community occupying communal land, the law discriminates against them by not giving them the right to ownership of land as individuals. The provision empowers the President to excise land from within the boundaries of a communal area. Once a declaration to that effect has been made, the land becomes State land which may then be granted, sold, or disposed of in any other manner under the Communal Land Act or any other law within the country. This provision gives the President the authority to pave the way for the ownership of such land in any of the methods described above. The law enables any person who so wishes to acquire as owner land that is no longer part of communal land.'

[9] (1995) 1 NWLR (Pt 372).

Another challenge for African courts is whether the continued occupation, ownership, and management of their lands constitute a public purpose in whatever form it is couched. The literature on law, policy, and practice surrounding the requirement of 'public purpose' as a fundamental requirement for the eminent domain in Africa[10] suggests inconsistencies in evaluating the adequacy of an asserted public purpose. In many cases, African courts have adopted an attitude of substantial deference to executive claims of fidelity to 'public purpose' and have subjected asserted public purpose to greater scrutiny in other cases.[11] An appropriate standard ensures that asserted claims of public purpose are correctly verified. The standards of 'rationality' and 'proportionality' are explored as appropriate standards that provide a broad spectrum for the appropriate review of the exercise of eminent domain and interrogate the connection between state action and underlying reasons, facts, and circumstances.

2.3 *Procedure for Compulsory Acquisition*

The dominant procedure for the compulsory acquisition of land includes publishing a notice of intention to acquire such land compulsorily and ensuring that the affected individual or community receives the notice for comments or objections and is given a stated period for comments. The procedure includes the availability for judicial review.

The idea of public participation as a crucial requirement in eminent domain is very recent and challenges the notion that eminent domain is expropriation without any involvement of the property owner, except with respect to compensation. Since the payment of compensation is regarded as an adequate limitation and safeguard of the awesome powers of the State, it is not surprising that the idea that property owners ought to be involved in the process of compulsory acquisition appears uninteresting. However, the idea of free, prior, and informed consent of indigenous communities in Africa regarding the expropriation of their ancestral lands has achieved significant milestones to the point that it may be regarded as a principle of indigenous land tenure management.[12] Two African regional pieces of jurisprudence anchor this principle. The African Commission on Human and Peoples' Rights in *Centre for Minority Rights Development (Kenya) and Minority Rights Group (on behalf of Endorois Welfare Council) v Republic of Kenya*[13] and the judgement of the African Court on Human and Peoples' Rights in the case of *African Commission on Human and Peoples' Rights v Republic of Kenya*,[14] interpret the United Nations

---

[10] See, for example, Wily (2018), pp. 77–104; Tagliarino (2016).

[11] See, for example, the Zambian Supreme Court in *Blerk v Attorney General* 2021 ZMSC 31.

[12] See Ndlovu, Nwauche (2022), pp. 201–227.

[13] Hereafter (2009) AHRLR 75 (ACHPR 2009) (*Endorois*).

[14] Application 006-2012. (hereafter *Ogiek*).

Declaration of the Rights of Indigenous Peoples (UNDRIP) which in Article 32 recognises the rights of indigenous peoples to determine and develop priorities and strategies for the development or use of their lands and territories. In addition, Articles 10,[15] 11(2),[16] 19,[17] 26,[18] and 38[19] of the UNDRIP reinforce the principle of free, prior, and informed consent in the management of communal indigenous land tenure. The Endorois, a traditional pastoralist community of approximately 60,000 people living in Lake Bogoria in central Kenya, were dispossessed of their traditional and ancestral lands in the 1970s to make way for a national reserve and tourist facilities. For centuries, the Endorois had established a sustainable way of life which was inextricably linked to their ancestral land. Their ownership of Lake Bogoria had remained unchallenged for centuries and was widely accepted by the surrounding tribes. During British colonial rule, the Endorois retained the right of possession and use of the land, although the ownership was vested in the British Crown. At Kenyan independence in 1963, the Endorois maintained their customary rights of use and possession over the land, although title was passed to the county council to be held on behalf of the Endorois community. The Kenyan government gazetted the area as a game reserve in 1973, and the Endorois were dispossessed of their ancestral land, allegedly without their FPIC. After being evicted from the fertile land around the lake, the Endorois were forced to congregate on arid land, where many of their cattle died. In their communication, the Endorois alleged that they had been forcefully dispossessed of their ancestral land in the Lake Bogoria area without proper prior consultation or adequate and effective compensation. The African Commission held that the forced removal of the Endorois people violated Article 14 of the African Charter on Human and Peoples' Rights[20] because the Kenyan state

---

[15] 'Indigenous peoples shall not be forcibly removed from their lands or territories. No relocation shall take place without the free, prior and informed consent of the indigenous peoples concerned and after agreement on just and fair compensation and, where possible, with the option of return.'

[16] 'States shall provide redress through effective mechanisms, which may include restitution, developed in conjunction with indigenous peoples, with respect to their cultural, intellectual, religious and spiritual property taken without their free, prior and informed consent or in violation of their laws, traditions and customs.'

[17] States shall consult and cooperate in good faith with the indigenous peoples concerned through their own representative institutions in order to obtain their free, prior and informed consent before adopting and implementing legislative or administrative measures that may affect them.

[18] (1) Indigenous peoples have the right to the lands, territories and resources which they have traditionally owned, occupied or otherwise used or acquired. (2) Indigenous peoples have the right to own, use, develop and control the lands, territories and resources that they possess by reason of traditional ownership or other traditional occupation or use, as well as those which they have otherwise acquired. (3) States shall give legal recognition and protection to these lands, territories and resources. Such recognition shall be conducted with due respect to the customs, traditions and land tenure systems of the indigenous peoples concerned.

[19] States in consultation and cooperation with indigenous peoples, shall take the appropriate measures, including legislative measures, to achieve the ends of this Declaration.

[20] Article 14 of the African Charter on Human and Peoples' Rights provides that the right to property shall be guaranteed and may only be encroached upon in the interest of public need or in the general interest of the community and in accordance with the provisions of appropriate laws.

had not ensured the effective participation of the Endorois community and their consent to the expropriation of their ancestral lands. The African Court on Human and Peoples' Rights in *Ogiek* considered the claim by an indigenous minority ethnic group in Kenya comprising approximately 20,000 members, 15,000 of whom inhabit the greater Mau Forest complex. It was determined that their right to property protected by Article 14 of the African Charter had been violated by the Kenya Forest Service, which issued a 30-day eviction notice in 2009 and had not obtained their free, prior, and informed consent. The African Court held that the lack of effective consultation and consent was in breach of Article 14 of the African Charter. As stated above, these two decisions represent the requirement of free, prior, and informed consent of indigenous communities in the expropriation of their indigenous land tenure. Several African states have elaborated different aspects of this principle through legislation and case law. For example, the 2017 Community Land Regulations of the Community Land Act set out a procedure for community consent to the compulsory acquisition of community land. Paragraph 15 of the Regulations recognises the fact that community land may be converted to public land by the Land Act and sets a procedure for the information and consultation of community members. A community land management committee shall present any notice of intention to compulsorily acquire part or the whole of the community land from the National Land Commission, in accordance with Section 131 of the Land Act, to the community assembly for information and any other direction on the matter regarding the compulsory acquisition process. Additionally, the community may, on its initiative, transfer, and surrender community land with the approval of two-thirds of the community's members. The silence of the Community Land Regulations on the consent of the community suggests that the Community Land Act recognises consultation and information to the community as adequate.

Recent case law from Kenya, such as *Patrick Musimba v The National Land Commission*,[21] suggests that consultation rather than the consent of indigenous communities would satisfy the principle of free, prior, and informed consent. In *Musimba*, the High Court of Kenya endorsed the procedure for acquiring land under the Land Act, which stipulates that acquisition notices be issued as part of a consultation process, but does not require the consent of the landholder. Under the Land Act, the National Land Act issues a notice of acquisition in a gazette and conducts an inquiry to ascertain proprietary interests and determine compensation. The idea of obtaining the consent of indigenous communities regarding the expropriation of their lands can be seen in different cases including *County Government of Turkana v National Land Commission*[22] where the appellants challenged two Gazette Notices (dated 8/2/2019 and 15/2/2019) published by the National Land Commission, where notices were given on behalf of the National Government declaring the National Government's intention to acquire land for the development of petroleum oil and the LAPSSET Corridor. Turkana County comprises mainly unadjudicated land

[21] [2016] eKLR.

[22] [2020] KECA 89 (eKLR).

occupied by the predominantly pastoralist Turkana community and is thus community land within the meaning of Article 63 of the Constitution of Kenya and the Community Land Act 2016. The respondents were alleged to have disregarded the Constitution, the Land Act No. 6 of 2012, and the Community Land Act 2016 and failed to engage the appellant in the acquisition process. The two petitions raised related issues concerning the acquisition of land within Turkana County, because there was no public participation or consultations between the National Government and County Governments, on the one hand, and the inhabitants of Turkana County, on the other, before the issuance of the said notices. After hearing the rival positions presented by the appellant and the respondents, the trial judge held that the entire dispute boiled down to a dispute over land acquisition in Turkana County, which matter was not ripe for litigation. Furthermore, the judge ruled against the appellant for failing to invoke the internal dispute resolution mechanism provided under the Inter-Governmental Relations Act and Article 189 of the Constitution, which provides an alternative dispute resolution mechanism as a first step in disputes involving national and county governments or between counties before filing judicial proceedings. The matter remained a point of contention for a while, even though established principles of public participation, such as access to information, arguably should determine how the National Land Commission consults with indigenous communities.[23] These principles have been confirmed in *Lorunyei & Another v Attorney General & 3 Others*, where the petition challenged the decision of the National Land Commission (NLC) and the County Government of Samburu to allocate Turkana community land in Kawap and Suguta Valley to the Kenya Defence Forces (KDF) in exchange for land in Maralal. The Samburu community had successfully lobbied for the return of its ancestral land in Maralal, prompting the third respondent, County Government of Samburu, NLC, and the Ministry of Defence to exchange it for the Turkana community's land in Kawap without consultation. The petitioners claimed a violation of their rights to equality, property, and fair administrative action. The court held that the suit land was community land; that the respondents' actions amounted to compulsory acquisition without due process and compensation; that failure to involve the Turkana community violated the principle of public participation; and that Gazette Notice No. 2080 of 2021, which allocated the suit land to the KDF, was unconstitutional. The court finally held that the process of annexation of the suit land by the NLC on behalf of the KDF was unlawful for violating Articles 10, 27, 40, 47, and 56 of the Constitution of Kenya.

South African courts have also interpreted what meaningful consultation means in a series of decisions concerning the environmental rights of indigenous communities. In *Sustaining the Wild Coast NPC and Others v Minister of Mineral Resources and Energy and Others*,[24] the Eastern Cape High Court set aside an exploration permit because of a failure of meaningful consultation with the affected indigenous

[23] See, for example, *Mui Coal Basin Local Community v Permanent Secretary Ministry of Energy* [2015] eKLR; *Abdalla v Attorney General* [2013] eKLR; and *Save Lamu v National Environmental Management Authority* [2019] eKLR.

[24] [2022] ZAECMKHC 55.

communities in the grant and renewal of an exploration right. In October 2021, the rights holders issued a notice of their intention to conduct a 3D seismic survey along the south-eastern coast of South Africa. The Court interdicted the survey because the grant and renewal of the exploration right violated the Promotion of Administrative Justice Act of 2000 for procedural unfairness. After all, the permit holder had failed to adequately consult with interested and affected communities. The permit holders had consulted with the monarchs of various communities but not with the community members, and further, the notice of the exploration right had been provided in the English and Afrikaans languages, rather than in Xhosa, the language spoken by the majority of members of the affected communities.[25]

The concept of meaningful consultation falls short of a requirement for free, informed, and prior consent, which is often a statutorily based requirement for free, prior, and informed consent of indigenous communities in the expropriation of their land tenure.[26] Ultimately, all African states need to comply with is a notice to indigenous communities of an intention to expropriate their land.

2.4 *Payment of Compensation*

The prompt payment of compensation appears to have crystallised into a general principle of compulsory acquisition.[27] However, given the socio-cultural and identitarian significance of indigenous land tenure to such communities, determining adequate compensation for communal land is considerably difficult. How does a court assess long-standing occupation and the significance of ancestral lands for an indigenous community? Even where relocation is possible.

A developing discourse in the area of compulsory acquisition is whether compensation should be paid before the state takes possession of the land. Concerning the time of payment of compensation, Ugandan courts have interpreted Section 26(2) of the 1995 Constitution (as amended)[28] to hold that, despite the provisions of Section 7 of the Land Acquisition Act, the state should pay full, prompt, and adequate compensation before possession of expropriated land.[29] The Ugandan position varies from the law and practice of compulsory acquisition in other African

[25] See generally in *Maledu and Others v Itereleng Bagatla Mineral Resources (Pty) Ltd and Another* 2019 (2) SA 1 (CC).

[26] See, for example, the case of *Bengwenyama Minerals (Pty) Ltd v Genorah Resources (Pty) Ltd* [2010] ZACC 26 that established a duty of meaningful consultation with respect to the grant of an exploration right in the framework of the Mineral and Petroleum Resources Development Act.

[27] See, for example, sect 20(1)(a) of the Ghana Constitution that provides for the prompt payment of compensation.

[28] 'No person shall be compulsorily deprived of property or any interest in or right over property of any description except where there is prompt payment of fair and adequate compensation, prior to the taking of possession or acquisition of the property.'

[29] See Muhwezi v Uganda National Roads Authority [2023] UGHC 142.

countries. Considerable opposition to this principle in Uganda led to a failed government Bill allowing possession of expropriated land before compensation payment.[30]

Another developing issue is the idea that certain objectives of expropriation, such as land reform and redistribution, can overrule the payment of compensation for expropriation. The expropriation of private land without compensation by the Zimbabwean government in the 1980s brought the issue to the fore,[31] including a long-litigated history.[32] In South Africa, Section 25(8) of the Constitution mandates land reform '... to redress the results of past racial discrimination'. Although the attempt to amend Section 25 of the Constitution through the 18th Amendment to provide for expropriation without compensation recently collapsed, the principle that expropriation without compensation is a desirable and defensible principle for many purposes, including the redistribution of land, is worthy of investigation. Several constitutions list circumstances of compulsory property acquisition by operation of law and do not entitle the property owner to compensation or even adequate compensation. For example, Article 16(1) of the Zambian Constitution provides that:

> 16 (1) Except as provided in this Article no property of any description shall be compulsorily taken possession of, and he interest in or right over property of any description shall be compulsorily acquired unless by or under the authority of an Act of parliament which provides for payment of adequate compensation for the property or interest or right to be taken possession of or acquired.

Article 16(2) lists several matters[33] that appear ambiguous because they could be construed as qualifying the general provision in Article 16(1) so that all deprivation must conform to the tenor of the clauses. Another understanding is that the matters

---

[30] See Muhindo (2017).

[31] See, for example, Tsabora (2016), pp. 213–229; Richardson (2004); Dancaescu (2003), pp. 615–644; Scoones et al. (2010).

[32] See, for example, *Mike Campbell (Pvt) Ltd v Republic of Zimbabwe* [2008] SADCT 2.

[33] These matters are: — a. in satisfaction of any tax, rate or due; b. by way of penalty for breach of any law, whether under civil process or after conviction of an offence; c. in execution of judgements or orders of courts; d. upon the attempted removal of the property in question out of or into Zambia in contravention of any law; e. as an incident of a contract including a lease, tenancy, mortgage, charge, pledge or bill of sale or of a title deed to land; f. for the purpose of its administration, care or custody on behalf of and for the benefit of the person entitled to the beneficial interest therein; g. by way of the vesting of enemy property or for the purpose of the administration of such property; h. for the purpose of— i. the administration of the property of a deceased person, a person of unsound mind or a person who has not attained the age of eighteen years, for the benefit of the persons entitled to the beneficial interest therein; ii. the administration of the property of a person adjudged bankrupt or a body corporate in liquidation, for the benefit of the creditors of such bankrupt or body corporate and, subject thereto, for the benefit of other persons entitled to the beneficial interest in the property; iii. the administration of the property of a person who has entered into a deed of arrangement for the benefit of his creditors; or iv. vesting any property subject to a trust in persons appointed as trustees under the instrument creating the trust or by a court or, by order of a court, for the purpose of giving effect to the trust; i. in consequence of any law

listed in Article 16(2) are exceptions to the requirement of compensation in Article 16(1). The Zambian Supreme Court has adopted the latter interpretation in *Zambia National Holdings and United National Independence Party v The Attorney General*,[34] where it stated that:

---

relating to the limitation of actions; j. in terms of any law relating to abandoned, unoccupied, unutilised or undeveloped land, as defined in such law; k. in terms of any law relating to absent or non-resident owners, as defined in such law, of any property; l. in terms of any law relating to trusts or settlements; m. by reason of the property in question being in a dangerous state or prejudicial to the health or safety of human beings, animals or plants; n. as a condition in connection with the granting of permission for the utilisation of that or other property in any particular manner; o. for the purpose of or in connection with the prospecting for or exploitation of, minerals belonging to the Republic on terms which provide for the respective interests of the persons affected; p. in pursuance of a provision of the marketing of property of that description in the common interests of the various persons otherwise entitled to dispose of that property; q. by way of the taking of a sample for the purposes of any law; r. by way of acquisition of the shares, or a class of shares, in a body corporate on terms agreed to by the holders of not less than nine-tenths in value of those shares or that class of shares; s. where the property consists of an animal, upon its being found trespassing or straying; . for so long as may be necessary for the purpose of any examination, investigation, trial or inquiry or, in the case of the land, the carrying out thereon— i. of work for the purpose of the conservation of natural resources or any description; or • Protection of environment ii. of agricultural development or improvement which the owner or occupier of the land has been required, and has without reasonable and lawful excuse refused or failed, to carry out; u. where the property consists of any licence or permit; v. where the property consists of wild animals existing in their natural habitat or the carcasses of wild animals; w. where the property is held by a body corporate established by law for public purposes and in which no moneys have been invested other than moneys provided by Parliament; x. where the property is any mineral, mineral oil or natural gases or any rights accruing by virtue of any title or licence for the purpose of searching for or mining any mineral, mineral oil or natural gases— i. upon failure to comply with any provision of such law relating to the title or licence or to the exercise of the rights accruing or to the development or exploitation of any mineral, mineral oil or natural gases; or ii. in terms of any law vesting any such property or rights in the President; y. for the purpose of the administration or disposition of such property or interest or right by the President in implementation of a comprehensive land policy or of a policy designed to ensure that the statute law, the Common Law and the doctrines of equity relating to or affecting the interest in or rights over land, or any other interests or right enjoyed by Chiefs and persons claiming through and under them, shall apply with substantial uniformity throughout Zambia; z. in terms of any law providing for the conversion of titles to land from freehold to leasehold and the imposition of any restriction on subdivision, assignment or subletting; aa. in terms of any law relating to— i. the forfeiture or confiscation of the property of a person who has left Zambia for the purpose or apparent purpose, of defeating the ends of justice; ii. the imposition of a fine on, and the forfeiture or confiscation of the property of, a person who admits a contravention of any law relating to the imposition or collection of any duty or tax or to the prohibition or control of dealing or transactions in gold, currencies, or securities.

[34] (1994) SJ 22(SC).

Article 16(1) clearly states the general rule, that is, the acquisition must be under a law which must provide for adequate compensation. Subarticle (2) on the other hand goes on to give exceptions to, and not categories of, the general rule. It deals with situations where an involuntary loss of property could take place even without adequate or any compensation.[35]

2.5 *Subsequent Use of Compulsorily Acquired Indigenous Land*

Another safeguard for indigenous communities is a requirement that the use of compulsorily acquired land is for its stated purpose. For example, Article 20(5) of the Ghana Constitution states that: 'Any property compulsorily taken possession of or acquired in the public interest or for a public purpose shall be used only in the public interest or for the public purpose for which it was acquired (6) Where the property is not used in the public interest or for the purpose for which it was acquired, the owner of the property immediately before the compulsory acquisition, shall be given the first option for acquiring the property and shall, on such re-acquisition refund the whole or part of the compensation paid to him as provided for by law or such other amount as is commensurate with the value of the property at the time of the re-acquisition'. In the same breadth, Article 22(6) of the Gambia Constitution provides that: 'Where any property is not used in the public interest or for the public purpose for which it was taken or acquired, the person who was the owner immediately before the compulsory taking or acquisition shall be given the first option of acquiring that property'.

3 Have African Judiciaries and Governments Failed Indigenous Peoples in the Large-Scale Acquisition of Indigenous Lands?

The eminent domain of African states has enabled the large-scale acquisition of their land tenure through compulsory acquisition and reduced available land, ultimately affecting the community's ability to consider the prospects of privatisation of their land tenure. One of the subtle consequences of compulsory acquisition is a disposition towards the voluntary disposition of indigenous communal land in Africa. Although it is difficult to measure how the possibility of compulsory acquisition could cause indigenous communities to negotiate the sale or lease of their lands, the widespread acquisition of such lands across Africa suggests that African governments are somewhat involved in such disposition, even if tacitly.

---

[35] Ibid at p 29.

The considerable literature on the state's inability to protect indigenous communities in the large-scale acquisition of indigenous lands attributes the weak capacity of African states[36] to mitigate the large-scale acquisition of indigenous land but neglects to consider whether the large-scale acquisition of indigenous lands is an objective of public policy. The fact that access to indigenous land tenure is an objective of the privatisation programme anchored on the statutory and constitutional reform of indigenous land tenure should imagine large-scale acquisition of indigenous land tenure as a form of privatisation. There is little doubt that strong African states may not only have prevented large-scale acquisition but also negotiated better terms of acquisition. The fact remains that the belief that indigenous land tenure should be reformed is likely to disfavour substantial state involvement.

4 Conclusion

Although it is difficult to imagine why a state's eminent domain should not extend to indigenous land tenure, ensuring that the procedural safeguards in the compulsory acquisition of land are followed ensures the protection of indigenous land tenure. A substantive requirement of the prior informed consent of indigenous communities ensures that compulsory measures have a minimal impact on indigenous communities.[37] A favourable future for indigenous law in Africa is ensured if African states were to sparingly acquire indigenous land tenure.

References

Boone C (2015) Land tenure regimes and state structure in rural Africa: implications for forms of resistance to large-scale land acquisitions by outsiders. J Contemp Afr Stud 33(2):171–190. https://doi.org/10.1080/02589001.2015.1065576

Cotula L (2012) 'Land grabbing' in the shadow of the law: Legal frameworks regulating the global land rush. Edward Elgar Publishing, Cheltenham

Dancaescu N (2003) Note: land reform in Zimbabwe. Florida J Int Law 15:615–644

Muhindo J (2017) Compulsory land acquisition in Uganda: An analysis of the proposed amendment of Article 26 of the Constitution, Kampala. ACODE Policy Briefing Paper Series No. 47

Ndlovu N, Nwauche ES (2022) Free prior and informed consent in Kenyan law after *Endorois* and *Ogiek*. Cambridge University Press, London, pp 201–227

Nyarko MG (2019) The right to property and compulsory land acquisition in Ghana: a human rights perspective. Afr J Int Comp Law 101:100–125

Richardson CJ (2004) The collapse of Zimbabwe in the wake of the 2000–2003 land reforms. The Edwin Mellen Press, Lewiston

Scoones I, Marongwe N, Mavedzenge B, Mahenehene J, Murimbarima F, Sukume C (2010) Zimbabwe's land reform: myths and realities. James Currey, Oxford

[36] See for example Boone (2015), pp. 171–190.; Cotula (2012).

[37] See, for example, Wily (2018), pp. 77–103.

Tagliarino NK (2016) Encroaching on land and livelihoods: How national expropriation laws measure up against international standards. World Resources Institute and University of Groningen working paper.
Tsabora J (2016) Reflections on the constitutional regulation of property and land rights under the 2013. Zimbabwean Const J Afr Law 60:213–229
Wily L (2018) Compulsory acquisition as a constitutional matter. J Afr Law 62:77–104

Documentation and Registration of Indigenous Land Tenure

Contents

1 Introduction 113
2 State Practice in the Documentation and Registration of Indigenous Land Tenure 115
3 Issues from State Practice 121
3.1 Significant Orally Held Communal Indigenous Land Tenure in Africa 122
3.2 Establishing an Indigenous Land Records Registry 122
3.3 Abdication of Indigenous Communities of their Obligation to Record their Indigenous Land Tenure 123
3.4 Consulting Traditional Authorities in Documenting and Registering Indigenous Land Tenure 123
4 Conclusion 123
References 124

1 Introduction

The oral nature of indigenous law results in indigenous land tenure that is undocumented in several African states. If indigenous law exists irrespective of its manifestation, it follows from this that written aspects of indigenous law simply represent another form of indigenous law. Across Africa, the widespread belief that indigenous land tenure is orally held sustained a conceptual obstacle to the idea that documented indigenous land tenure is also indigenous land tenure. As noted in chapter "The Privatisation of Indigenous Land Tenure Development and the Future of African Indigenous Law" of this book, documenting indigenous land tenure was a necessary condition for the reform of indigenous land tenure.[1] In fact, that gap has been a significant drawback to the privatisation process, and in many communities, the fact that privatisation has led to documentation of some indigenous land tenure amid orally held indigenous land tenure is a concern. Documentation should be a fundamental construct of indigenous land tenure, and no effort should be spared to

[1] See Orani and Schermers (2017).

E. Nwauche, *The Privatisation of Indigenous Land Tenure and the Future of African Indigenous Law*, https://doi.org/10.1007/978-3-032-14881-0_6

allow communities to document their land tenure. Indeed, the survival of indigenous land tenure is dependent on the documentation of that tenure. The privatisation of indigenous land tenure is likely to proceed better if there are written records of a community's land tenure and dealings. Documentation is important for indigenous communities to negotiate how their tenure becomes an object of economic relationships as social forces of the urbanisation process, population growth, changes in the food system, international land grabbing, and climate change, among others, erupt around them. Indigenous communities are capable of building economic relationships themselves to partly address the objectives of privatisation.

Since indigenous land tenure is held orally, it should not be a cumbersome process for indigenous communities to reflect their land tenure in a written document. Documentation should not involve norm-making, but rather a reflection of the multiple concurrent and interlocking interests over indigenous land tenure. This chapter distinguishes documentation from the orthodox registration of instruments of land title transfer, which is a feature of the property regime in several African states. Land registration is often a state project and important because it is evidence of title with which the benefits of individualised land tenure can be secured, for example, in credit and tax purposes. However, documentation is crucial for registration and can exist independently of the latter. While a state ponders on how to provide evidence of indigenous land tenure through a secure database that is in use for statutory land tenure in several African countries; what the privatisation of indigenous land tenure has achieved in several African countries is to show that documentation of indigenous land tenure is grossly inadequate and making the documentation and registration of indigenous land tenure a fundamental part of the reform process. It seems natural to expect African states to be leading the documentation of indigenous land tenure, especially as several land tenure privatisation legislations provide for such an important exercise. The available evidence over the years has often shown a lack of political will and inadequate resources to effectively document indigenous land tenure in several African states[2] such as Ghana,[3] Botswana, and Kenya. Without documentation, it has often been difficult for land registration especially where registration is tied to the registration of instruments of land transfer and other technical standards that may ordinarily be incompatible with the oral nature of indigenous land tenure.

How far have African states fared in the documentation of indigenous land tenure? Unfortunately, the answer is: not far enough. Scholarly reflection of state-led documentation and registration processes is resoundingly negative in many respects[4] but also positive in respect of other initiatives that are often localised in different states, regions, and communities across Africa.[5] What has emerged is a sustained

---

[2] See, for example, Toulmin (2005), pp 27–54.

[3] See, for example, Abdulai (2010).

[4] See for example Coldham (1985) as well as Barry and Danso (2014).

[5] See for example, Abab et al. (2021)

commitment to document communal indigenous land tenure, which bodes well for the future of communal indigenous land tenure in Africa.

2 State Practice in the Documentation and Registration of Indigenous Land Tenure

In this section, this chapter reviews the provisions for land documentation and registration, as well as evidence of this practice in several African states.

Ghana recognises the importance of recording and registering of indigenous land tenure and recognises three systems of recording and registering of land and land interests. The first includes the recording of customary interests and rights by the Customary Land Secretariats. The second system is the registration of instruments relating to land, and the third system is the registration of title, interests, and rights in land. The interests in land that can be registered include allodial title, as well as customary freehold, customary leasehold, usufructuary interest, leasehold interests, and customary tenancy. These are the primary interests in land and include the tenure of indigenous land of communal and individual standing. The holders of these primary interests are entitled to register secondary interests in land, such as mortgages, easements, restrictive covenants, profit a prendre, power of attorney, and contractual licenses. Of importance is the fact that community and family land are registrable by virtue of Section 182 of the GLA. A survey plan prepared with the assistance of the Director of Survey is important for an application to register a community of family land and for any alienation of part of the community or family land.[6] A disposition of community or family land can only be legal and entitled to be registered if the requisite consent and concurrence are given and the approval of the Regional Lands Commission is obtained.[7] Interestingly, Section 267(5) of the Constitution prohibits the creation of a freehold interest in community land even as Section 2 of the GLA defines an allodial interest as including those who purchase the allodial title. Where there are customary interests, the functions of the Customary Land Secretariat established by the stool, skin, clan, or families that own communal indigenous land in accordance with Section 14(1) of the GLA include the recording of these interests in land and keeping an accurate record of land transactions with respect to the community and family land. The records of the secretariat are evidence of transactions and serve as notice,[8] but individuals with customary interests do not qualify as holding privatised interests in land. A reading of Ghana's Land Commission Act of 2008 and the GLA reinforces the position that there is one registration system for Ghana with a supplementary customary record system. Land conflicts and litigation in the indigenous land tenure system in Ghana have arisen

[6] See sect 182(4) of the GLA.

[7] See sect 267 of the Constitution of Ghana.

[8] See sect 15(2) of the GLA.

from the incapacity of the Customary Land Secretariates and the Land Commission.[9] From the perspective of the future of indigenous law, the requirement of writing as evidence of customary transactions should be welcomed. Additionally, indigenous land tenure in the form of allodial ownership is also registrable. These facts sustain the privatisation of indigenous land tenure, but also the fact that such privatisation can occur within the framework of indigenous land tenure through the imposition of customary burdens and obligations recognised by indigenous land tenure.

As noted in chapter "Models of Private Interests in Indigenous Land Tenure in Africa", dealing with the management of indigenous land tenure in Kenya, the registration of a community under the Kenyan Community Land Act is required before a community can be considered the owner of indigenous land as a body corporate.[10] The regulations governing registrations require notice and adjudication of land claims and settlement of boundaries before a title is issued in the name of the community. Certificates of customary land use and occupancy are entered in the Community Land Registers. Section 8 of Kenya's Land Registration Act 2012 provides for a Community Land Register that should contain a cadastral map showing the extent of the community land and identified areas of common interest; the name of the community identified in accordance with Article 63(1) of the Constitution and any other law relating to community land; a register of members of the community; the user of the land; the identity of those members registered as group representatives; the names and identity of the members of the group. The Registrar shall issue a certificate of title or certificate of lease in the prescribed form and shall not register any instrument purporting to dispose of rights or interests in community land except in accordance with the law relating to community land. The certificate issued by the Registrar is deemed by all courts as *prima facie* evidence that 'the person named as proprietor of the land is the absolute and indefeasible owner, subject to the encumbrances, easements, restrictions and conditions contained or endorsed in the certificate, and the title of that proprietor shall not be subject to challenge, except on the ground of fraud or misrepresentation to which the person is proved to be a party; or (b) where the certificate of title has been acquired illegally, unprocedurally or through a corrupt scheme'.[11]

In Angola, Presidential Order 14/18 created a Commission to register rural land for communities linked to the implementation of the 'My Land' programme to strengthen communal tenure rights. The Angolan government reports that several communities have been registered and are undergoing the process.[12] Mozambique is not left out, and there are

[9] See, for example, Abubakari et al. (2018), pp. 539–554; Edwin et al. (2020), p. 416; Kuusaana et al. (2013), pp. 14–27.

[10] See the case of *Cheub Adan Ali v Community Land Registrar, North Eastern Region Mandera* [2021] where the Court held that the constitutional rights of a community become live on the registration of the community. Paragraph 8(1) of the Community Land Regulations 2017.

[11] See the case of *Lucia Kariuki v Grace Wanjuru* [2022] eKLR.

[12] See De Satgé (2022).

> Several projects have tested or are testing this 'local documentation' approach and the 'local land register' model in diverse situations, across nearly 100 communities covering more than 125,000 hectares. Some 50,000 locally issued certificates, confirming individual or household DUAT rights, have been issued by these communities, represented by legally registered associations.[13]

Ethiopia's federal land use laws have provided for the registration of rural land. First, the Federal Democratic Republic of Ethiopia Rural Land Administration and Use Proclamation of 2005 provides in Article 6 that the size of rural lands under the holdings of private persons, communities, governmental, and non-governmental organisations shall be measured as appropriate using cultural and modern measurement equipment; their land use and level of fertility shall be registered by the competent authorities established at all levels. Any holder of rural land shall be given a holding certificate to be prepared by the competent authority, which indicates the size of the land, land use type and cover, level of fertility and borders, as well as the obligations and rights of the holder. Article 6 of the AFAR National Regional State Rural Land Administration and Use Proclamation No. 49/2009 provides for the surveying and registering of pastoral communal lands and issuing communal holding certificates for communal lands that are held communally by pastoralists shall be surveyed, registered, and certificates of holdings issued in the name of the community using such communal lands. The details will be determined in the regulation. The communal land holding certificate shall be deposited with the representative of the community/clan of the holder of the land. Ethiopia's recent Rural Land Administration and Use Proclamation of 2024 declares that registration of rural land shall be compulsory, systematic, and parcel-based.[14] Article 44 states that the assignment of a unique parcel identification number shall be given in order of descending government administrative structure and shall fulfil the following features: a unique parcel identification number that is permanent even during the exchange and transfer of holdings, except in cases of division and amalgamation of holdings. The unique parcel identification number shall contain a regional identification that shall be represented by two letters; a zonal identification that shall be represented by two numbers; a woreda identification that shall be represented by two numbers; a kebele identification that shall be represented by three numbers, making a parcel identification of five numbers. It is not surprising that Proclamation 2024 links different rural cadastral surveying methods to the national geodetic ground control points.

In Nigeria, there is no requirement for localised documentation of customary land tenure. Land registration legislation[15] does not specifically refer to customary

---

[13] See Norfolk et al. (2020), p. 2.

[14] See Article 43 of the 2024 Proclamation.

[15] See, for example, Land Instrument Registration Law Cap 72 Laws of Eastern Nigeria 1963, sect 2 (now re-enacted into the Land Instrument Registration Laws of all the states created from the defunct Eastern Region of Nigeria); Land Registration Law Cap 58 Laws of Northern Nigeria 1963, sect 2 (now re-enacted into the Land Instrument Registration Law of all the states created from the defunct Northern Region of Nigeria including the Abuja Federal Capital Territory).

rights of occupancy. However, in Nigerian land markets, there is practice for instruments evidencing the sale or assignment of customary rights of occupancy to be registered in state land registration registries. The lack of a mandate to document indigenous land tenure in Nigeria is unfortunate and continues the falsehood that orality is a feature of indigenous land tenure. Unfortunately, the documentation of indigenous land tenure is not a feature of the statutory land reform in Nigeria. One of the States of the Nigerian federation, Lagos State, has passed new legislation that is argued have negated the ambiguity whether certificates of occupancy are registrable in Nigeria.[16] Section 1 of the Lagos State Land Registration Law of 2015 defines 'document' as including 'any deed, judgment, decree, order, other document in writing requiring or capable of registration under the Law and includes a certificate of occupancy'. Section 2 provides that 'every document of interest or title to land in Lagos State shall be registered in accordance with the provisions of this law'. Section 26(1) further provides: 'Any holder in possession of any registrable document shall register it within sixty (60) days after obtaining the Governor's consent where applicable. The forms for registration of titled land and land covered by deeds/certificate of occupancy are contained in Forms 1 and 2 in Schedule 1 to this law'.

In Tanzania, a significant feature of the statutory reform of the tenure of indigenous land in Tanzania is the strong emphasis on the documentation of village land that includes communal and individual titles. The documentation process includes establishing village boundaries, creating village land use plans, and registering land in the Village Land Registry pursuant to Section 21 of the Act, which establishes a Village Land Registry. Furthermore, the Village Act provides for the registration and issuing of 'Certificates of Customary Right of Occupancy' of village land that reflect the cultural economic relationships of land tenure in Tanzanian villages. Registration of village land occurs after the adjudication of village land which enables the Village Council to resolve boundary disputes. The Tanzanian government is involved in the process of implementing the documentation of village land.[17] An example of this process includes the Guidelines for Participatory Village Land Use Planning Administration and Management in Tanzania, issued by the National Land Commission,[18] which has guided the documentation of village land use. Scholarly commentary on the utility of the process raises socio-economic and cultural issues with the 'participatory' process of the documentation of village land but notes the importance of completing the land use plan so that the villages could issue individual Certificates of Customary Rights of Occupancy.[19]

In chapter "Models of Private Interests in Indigenous Land Tenure in Africa" of this work, we note that communal land tenure exists in South Africa and that communities and families have a variety of legal instruments to secure their title and

[16] See, for example, Odionu and Oraegbunam (2021), pp. 50–54.

[17] See, for example, Schrieber (2017).

[18] National Land Use Planning Commission (2012).

[19] See Huggins (2016).

ultimately the title of any privatised land holding that emerges from such communal and family land holding. To that extent, the CPAs and other legal mechanisms secure the titles of indigenous land tenures. Tenurial tensions in South Africa continue over whether individuals should have the right to communal land tenure, such as those represented by the CPAs and other legal forms. The right to land tenure and security, therefore, was an object of the failed Communal Land Rights Act of 2004. The Communal Land Tenure Bill of 2017 was introduced to remedy perceived deficiencies, illustrating what can be achieved in South Africa. First, Clause 12 of that Bill requires that communal land must be registered in the name of a community or a name preferred by the community and where the community land has been subdivided, such land must also be registered in the name of a community member allocated the land or occupying same at the commencement of the proposed Act or in the name of a community member and the community if usufructuary rights and leases are involved. Certain conditions are attached to the registration of community land at the deeds registry and include that communal land designated as economic, social, environmental and infrastructural, developmental, pastoral, recreational, and for socio-economic objectives cannot be sold, donated, leased, encumbered, or in any manner disposed of without a written resolution to that effect supported by 60% of households of the relevant community.[20] Where communal land is subdivided for residential, agricultural, industrial, or commercial purposes, such land cannot be sold, donated, or in any other manner alienated to a person who is not a member of that community without offering members of the owner's family, members of the relevant community, or the state, the first option to acquire such subdivided portion.[21] Clause 14 of the Bill requires that all registrable transactions in respect of communal land must be registered in terms of this Act, the Deeds Registries Act, and any other applicable laws. There is considerable literature in South Africa on different options in the documentation and registration of communal land. Pienaar, for example, believes that:

> The main aim of a formalised structure should not be the individualisation of communal land tenure in the form of a freehold title to be used by communities as collateral for financial support, but the security offered by information (recording and publication) of communal land rights exercised within accepted community structures. The existing deeds registration system already provides for different forms of registration, namely individualised land rights in the case of surveyed land and urban fragmented property holding in the case of sectional titles and time-sharing (see section II above). It is possible to develop a third form to record communal land rights in the name of communities, in accordance with the distinct nature of community structures and communal land tenure (see section III above). The aim of such a register should be the recording of use rights associated with communal land tenure, which will provide the necessary information (publication) for the development of a comprehensive land administration system that is lacking at this stage. The information system should be upgradeable to provide for the registration of communal title and eventually individual title if required by a community.[22]

[20] See Clause 13 of the Bill.

[21] Ibid.

[22] Pienaar (2011), pp. 238–271, 258.

Evidence of the need for reform of the record keeping of communal land tenure in South Africa is found in the Final Report of the Presidential Advisory Panel on Land Reform and Agriculture.[23] That report proposed a Land Records Bill[24] to allow those who hold property 'off-register' to record and register their property using 'low-cost technologies and blockchain options'[25] to provide for 'local and accessible recordal of existing land rights, those rights held as individuals, households, extended families and communities'.[26] While national legislation is waiting or on its way, the idea of localised recording of communal land tenure is an attractive option. There is evidence of localised systems of land record keeping[27] across South Africa that could act as an inspiration for communal land record keeping, as South Africa makes its move towards a communal land rights framework.[28] One means by which customary land tenure may be strengthened is to encourage communities to produce a record of family and communal land as an adjunct to the community protocols.

In Uganda, a 2021 project titled 'Community-Based Land Registration and Land Use Planning on Customary Land' illustrates the challenges Uganda has faced with customary land documentation and registration since the land reform process of the 1990s. Under the Land Act of 1998, customary land registration is the responsibility of the Area Land Committees and the Recorder, and at district level by the District Land Board. Section 6(1) of the Land Act provides that a person, family, or community holding land under customary tenure on public land shall acquire a certificate of customary ownership, and a member of the family is entitled to have an agreed portion transferred and registered to the applicant. The Land Regulations of 2004 provide for simple hand drawing of a sketch map after the boundaries of a piece of land have been tape-measured. The total area is only estimated, and the sketch is not drawn to scale. No spatial framework is needed, and there is no georeferencing, giving rise to the assertion of LANDNet Uganda that a fit-for-purpose approach is used to register customary land in Uganda[29] that includes 'four tools that have been piloted in the country to facilitate the documentation of land rights of the 70% of the supposedly un-surveyed land (mostly under customary tenure) so as to create a complete and coherent cadastre in a relatively short time. These tools are Systematic Land Adjudication and Certification (SLAAC), Solutions for Open Land Administration-Open Tenure (SOLA- Open Tenure), Social Tenure Domain Model (STDM) and Cadastre Register Inventory Saving Paper (CRISP)'.[30] LANDNet notes that while Uganda's National Land Information System is based on the Torrens system that captures the tenure systems of freehold, mailo, and lease-

[23] Final Report of the Presidential Advisory Panel on Land Reform and Agriculture 2019.

[24] See Delius, Beinart (2021), pp. 60–83.

[25] Ibid. p. 87.

[26] Ibid.

[27] See, for example, Barry and Kingwill (2020), pp. 1–34.

[28] Ibid.

[29] See LANDNet (2022).

[30] Ibid. p. 16.

hold, 'customary tenure is instead mapped, adjudicated and CCOs issued to people through procedures and techniques that do not meet the standards and requirements of the National Land Information System'.[31] While noting that the 'assessment of registration of customary land law and practices established that it was generally coherent with the general stages of land registration ... significant loopholes within these customary land registration processes undermine the quality of the outcome or document issued'.[32] The loopholes include deficiencies in the nature of surveying and mapping and the lack of state guarantee on the Customary Certificate of Ownership of the accuracy of the information on the certificate. Other deficiencies include the impression that the conversion of the CCO implies that it is weaker than the certificates of title to freehold, mailo, and leasehold, and lack of maintenance of the sub county land registries that support the work of the Area Land Committees that register Customary Certificates of Occupancy as well as the optional registration of customary rights and interests.[33] Some recommendations to improve the registration of customary land in Uganda include a hybrid system of land registration of customary land in Uganda anchored on the adoption of a Customary Land Registry Law that will 'detail all the clauses relating to the transfer of customary land and registration of certificates of customary title'.[34]

Sierra Leone's experience in the recording and registration of customary land concludes this survey as an example of the determination of African states to record and register customary land. Land for Life reports of a June 2025 launch of the pilot phase for the recording and registration of customary land facilitated by the Ministry of Lands, Housing, and Country Planning through Sierra Leone's Land Administration Project (SLLAP).[35] This exercise complements the 2022 Customary Land Act and, in its infancy, is emblematic of Africa's recent turn to consider the recording and registration of indigenous land seriously.

3 Issues from State Practice

The brief overview of the recording and registration of indigenous land tenure in Africa leads to some observations.

[31] Ibid. p. 18.

[32] Ibid. p. 19.

[33] Ibid. pp. 20–21.

[34] Ibid. p. 22.

[35] See Land For Life (2025).

3.1 *Significant Orally Held Communal Indigenous Land Tenure in Africa*

It is not surprising that a significant portion of the communal tenure of indigenous land is held orally within the knowledge base of indigenous communities and in states that associate indigenous land tenure as an orally held system. Opposition to the privatisation process intuitively embraces orality, since the recording and registering communal indigenous land tenure is a fundamental condition of tenure reform in several African states. The recorded and registered indigenous land, according to this logic, is no longer indigenous land tenure but state land. However, there is a surfeit of evidence that several tenure agendas are to retain communal indigenous land tenure in a recorded and registered form. As our discussions have shown, the character of what is indigenous is not the form in which the tenure is held, but the collective intergenerational title held in socially embedded solidarity that sustains indigenous communities. Recording and registering communal indigenous land tenure improves the security of the tenure and facilitates privatisation, especially if the latter is achieved with the consent and agreement of the community, which is increasingly becoming the preferred method of privatisation in Africa. If privatisation is not designed to destroy indigenous communities in Africa, it is important to note that several African states have devoted resources to achieve this objective. These efforts are in their infancy, but suggest a widespread orthodoxy that recording and registering indigenous land tenure is a fundamental objective. The survival of indigenous African communities is facilitated by secure land tenure arrangements. The principles of indigenous land tenure would be improved by documentation, especially if these communities document the resolution of land tenure disputes.

3.2 *Establishing an Indigenous Land Records Registry*

It is easy to conclude that establishing a national indigenous land registry is a worthy objective for documenting indigenous land tenure. Several states, such as Ghana, Uganda, and Tanzania, have entrusted indigenous community hierarchies to work with state authorities to document their tenure. A registry, if properly organised, could represent the primary and secondary rights at stake and enable community members to present the proof required for official and commercial purposes. Furthermore, indigenous communities would be empowered to adjudicate disputes and engage in long-term planning. Whether these registries should be independent or part of national registries is a policy decision that states can make according to their circumstances.

3.3 Abdication of Indigenous Communities of their Obligation to Record their Indigenous Land Tenure

The advent of low technologies coupled with localised recording of indigenous land tenure suggests that indigenous communities could easily assume some responsibility in recording their indigenous land tenure, which could facilitate alignment with national record and registration systems. To rely completely on the state to design and deploy land documentation instruments does not measure up to the standards of administration afforded by the ownership and management of indigenous land tenure. Although indigenous hierarchies often easily protect communal interests in land tenure, the prospects of privatisation and compulsory acquisition of their land make it critical for indigenous communities to invest in systematic land documentation.

3.4 Consulting Traditional Authorities in Documenting and Registering Indigenous Land Tenure

The importance of consulting traditional rulers in the process of registering customary land rights is by some means related to the point of these communities engaging in self-help documentation of their land tenure. For example, Acholi tribal chiefs in the case of *Okello Omorro v Attorney General of Uganda*,[36] emphasised the absurdity of the laws that set out a process for titling land without mandatory consultation with the respective clan heads and customary institutions. Although the Ugandan Supreme Court rejected this proposal, the importance of consulting traditional authorities in the registration of customary land is not a trivial matter, given their valuable role in customary guidance. Although they were unsuccessful, the fact that Ugandan land law encourages consultation with traditional authorities underscores the contention of the Acholi chiefs.

4 Conclusion

The documentation of indigenous land tenure addresses the idea that orality is a characteristic of indigenous land tenure. Indeed, it may be argued that privatisation has quickened the need for documentation, and this is evident in the duties entrusted to indigenous communities in Tanzania, Kenya, Uganda, and Ghana. Since indigenous land tenure can thrive better with appropriate documentation, it is likely that other African states, and hopefully indigenous communities, will devote resources to the documentation.

[36] 2023 UGCC 107.

References

Abab SA, Wakjira FS, Negash TT (2021) Determinants of the Land Registration Information System Operational Success: Empirical Evidence from Ethiopia. Land 10, 12:1394. https://doi.org/10.3390/land10121394

Abdulai RT (2010) Traditional landholding institutions in sub-Saharan Africa: the operation of traditional landholding institutions in sub-Saharan Africa: a case study of Ghana. Lambert Academic Publishing, Saarbrücken

Abubakari Z, Richter C, Zevenbergen J (2018) Exploring the 'implementation gap' in land registration: How it happens that Ghana's official registry contains mainly leaseholds. Land Use Policy 79:539–554

Barry M, Danso EK (2014) Tenure security, land registration and customary tenure in a peri-urban Accra community. Land Use Policy 39:358–365

Barry M, Kingwill R (2020) Evaluating the community land record system in Monwabisi Park informal settlement in the context of hybrid governance and organisational culture. Land 9(124):1–34

Coldham S (1985) A comparative study of land tenure legislation in Africa. Acta Juridica 1985:189–212

De Satgé R (2022) Angola: context and land governance. Available at https://landportal.org/book/narratives/2022/angola. Accessed 10 July 2023

Delius P, Beinart W (2021) Securing the land: from customary land tenure to registered titled land? In: Mabasa K, Mabasa B (eds) Land in South Africa: contested meanings and nation formation. Mistra, pp 60–83

Edwin D, Glover EF, Glover EGK (2020) When tradition meets modernity in land registration: evidence from Dagbon, Ghana. Land 9:416. https://doi.org/10.3390/land91110416

Huggins C (2016) Village land use planning and commercialization of land in Tanzania land governance for equitable and sustainable development (Research Brief 01). Available at https://www.landgovernance.org/wp-content/uploads/2019/10/20160301-LANDacResearchBrief-01 Tanzania1.pdf

Kuusaana ED, Kidido JK, Appiah MN, Mireku KO (2013) Alternative dispute resolution by chiefs and tendamba: a case study of Kumasi and Wa traditional areas. Ghana Surv 5:14–27

Land For Life (2025) Pilot Phase for Customary Land Registration Launched in Pakimassagbong Chiefdom, Bombali District. Available at https://landforlife.org.sl/pilot-phase-for-customary-land-registration-launched-in-pakimassagbong-chiefdom-bombali-district/. Accessed 22 Oct 2025

LandNet (2022) Establishment of a customary land registry in Uganda. Available at https://landnet.ug/landwatch/wp-content/uploads/2022/02/LandRegistration_IssuesPaper.pdf. Accessed 28 Oct 2025

National Land Use Planning Commission (2012) Guidelines for participatory village land use planning, administration and management in Tanzania. Available at https://acrobat.adobe.com/id/urn:aaid:sc:EU:794ee1ae-7400-459d-b567-0980951b7a5e. Accessed 22 Oct 2025

Norfolk S, Quan J, Mullins D (2020) Options for securing tenure and documenting land rights in Mozambique: a land policy & practice paper. Chatham UK, Legend, p 2. Available at https://landportal.org/sites/default/files/library/resources/Moz_Policy_Paper_0.pdf

Odionu IO, Oraegbunam IKE (2021) The status of certificate of occupancy under the Land Registration Law 2015 of Lagos State: a wake-up call on other states in Nigeria. Int J Comp Law Legal Philosophy 3(1):50–54

Orani M, Schermers J (2017) The recognition of the customary land rights: lessons from the Province of Bié in Angola. Available at https://landportal.org/library/resources/recognition-customary-land-rights-lessons-province-bie-angola. Accessed 22 October 2025

Pienaar G (2011) Land information as a tool for effective land administration and development. In: Pluralism and Development: Studies in Access to Property in Africa. Acta Juridica, 238–271, 258

Republic of South Africa Final Report of the Presidential Advisory Panel on Land Reform and Agriculture 2019. https://www.gov.za/sites/default/files/gcis_document/201907/panelreport-landreform_1.pdf. Accessed 1 Nov 2025

Schrieber L (2017) Registering Rural Rights: Village Land Titling in Tanzania, 2008-2017. Available at https://successfulsocieties.princeton.edu/publications/registering-rural-rights-village-land-titling-tanzania. Accessed 22 October 2025

Toulmin C (2005) Securing land and property rights in sub-Saharan Africa: the role of local institutions. Land Use Policy 26(1):27–54. https://doi.org/10.1016/j.landusepol.2008.07.006

Arbitration and Adjudication of Indigenous Land Tenure Disputes

Contents

1 Introduction ... 127
2 Family and Communal Arbitration over Indigenous Land Tenure in African States ... 128
3 Local Land Management Institutions and Dispute Settlement of Indigenous Land Tenure Disputes ... 131
4 The Unlimited Jurisdiction of State Courts Over Indigenous Land Tenure Disputes ... 133
5 Conclusion ... 138
References ... 138

1 Introduction

Since dispute settlement is an integral part of all tenure systems and has been a part of communal indigenous land tenure, an investigation of how dispute settlement has fared within the privatisation process in Africa can be viewed from different perspectives. From the perspective of states that recognise the privatisation of communal indigenous land tenure, it is important to determine how the transformation of tenure is managed and how that may affect the future of indigenous law. This can be achieved through indigenous authorities' dispute settlement processes, which include 'alternative' land management institutions that are largely independent of traditional authorities. Another perspective is that the privatisation of indigenous land tenure occurs in plural legal systems, which involve state courts that are often statutorily endowed to review the decisions of indigenous dispute settlement mechanisms and, in some cases, entertain original suits from litigants. The unlimited jurisdiction of state judicial power also extends to indigenous land tenure, and several state courts have adjudicated over indigenous land tenure issues. The interface of the indigenous and state systems is a classic case of legal pluralism in action and has been approached by several African states in different permutations. Given the extensive permutations of how several African states have approached the settlement of indigenous land tenure disputes, this chapter seeks to draw broad lessons from state practice to determine whether there is evidence of how indigenous land

E. Nwauche, *The Privatisation of Indigenous Land Tenure and the Future of African Indigenous Law*, https://doi.org/10.1007/978-3-032-14881-0_7

tenure systems have contributed to the development of indigenous law, although this objective may not have been paramount in the legislated reform process.

2 Family and Communal Arbitration over Indigenous Land Tenure in African States

Several African states recognise different forms of indigenous adjudicatory bodies as the first step to settling indigenous land disputes as a consequence of recognising indigenous law as the normative framework of indigenous communities.[1] These indigenous adjudicatory bodies include indigenous leadership in council functioning as judicial authorities; community and family heads, as well as legacy institutions, such as age grades, and social groups, such as market women and tradesmen. Given the importance of tenurial relationships, communal indigenous authorities are often at the centre of arbitrating tenurial contestations.

It would appear normal that indigenous authorities should be at the centre of the privatisation process, since privatisation is often consequential to the fundamental structures of their sustenance and identity. Since privatisation occurs through constitutional and legislative intervention, it appears that the belief that privatisation is antithetical to indigenous land tenure is encouraged in several African states and diminishes the importance of indigenous law and its authorities. Providing for dispute settlement in new or reformed state judicial institutions beyond the control and direction of indigenous authorities is often the norm. It does make sense that state judicial authorities are the best option in enforcing a change in tenurial relations that indigenous authorities are opposed to. Consequently, there is doubt that indigenous authorities have the capacity to promote the privatisation of indigenous tenure even though the maintenance of communal tenurial relations that become an issue because of privatisation may well be better handled by indigenous authorities in several countries.

Indigenous arbitrations are informal and organised around normative understandings of indigenous communities. Generally, their proceedings are informal, but they are not exclusive, and modern plural legal systems align indigenous arbitral bodies with the review and legitimacy of state judicial hierarchy. One key point that has been raised in the review and legitimacy of indigenous arbitration is the question of consent to these proceedings. The idea that indigenous arbitral bodies should not be coercive has been a bone of contention in several African countries. For example, Section 88 of the Land Act of Uganda recognises the jurisdiction of traditional authorities in disputes over customary tenure. In Zimbabwe, although the resolution of disputes amongst people in their communities in accordance with customary law is a constitutionally enshrined function of traditional leaders, controversy continues regarding the extent of this function, given that certain statutes

[1] See, for example, Asaaga (2021), pp. 10, 143.

appear to delineate the jurisdiction of chiefs. First, Section 282(2) of the Constitution gives traditional leaders authority, jurisdiction, and control over communal land and its inhabitants. It may be stated that this gives the Chiefs unlimited jurisdiction to use customary law in dispute resolution. In addition, Section 5(n) of the Traditional Leaders Act, which includes the duties of chiefs, to adjudicate and resolve land disputes, aligns with constitutional principles. However, Section 8 of the Communal Land Act vests the administration of communal land solely in the Rural District Councils, and Section 15 of the Customary Law and Local Courts Act sets the jurisdiction of chiefs in land disputes at odds with constitutional provisions. In addition, Section 16(1)(g) of the Customary Law and Local Courts Act provides that a local court shall have jurisdiction in any case where the claim is determinable by customary law in respect of land or other immovable property. Since local courts are primary courts presided over by a headman or other person appointed by the minister or by a person designated by the minister, and a community court is presided over by a chief or other person so appointed by the minister or his designated officer, chiefs are excluded from indigenous land tenure matters. In *Chihoro v Murombo*[2] and *Chigavakava v Waire*,[3] Zimbabwean courts engaged the apparent contradiction between Section 16(1)(g) of the Customary Law and Local Courts Act and Section 5 of the Traditional Leaders Act, holding that a chief acts within the purview of the Traditional Leaders Act by only entertaining disputes relating to land that does not involve the allocation of land. Allocation of land, in my considered view, involves the granting of rights, interest, and title to land to an individual, whereas the resolving of a land dispute includes the entertainment of a dispute between or amongst individuals regarding an already allocated piece of land.

Several African states suggest that indigenous arbitration is part of the alternative dispute settlement process. For example, Kenya's CLA provides that a registered community may use alternative methods of dispute resolution mechanisms, including traditional dispute and conflict resolution mechanisms where appropriate, for the purposes of settling disputes and conflicts involving community land.

Section 88 of Uganda's Land Act also recognises the capacity of traditional authorities to act as mediators. In fact, the Land Tribunals can refer any matter before it to traditional authorities as mediators in any matter concerning customary tenure. Ghanaian Customary Land Secretariats have also extensively used alternative dispute resolution strategies to resolve tenure conflicts and typify through their adherence to Ghana's Alternative Dispute Resolution Act 2010, the idea that indigenous arbitration is part of alternative dispute resolution.[4]

In Ethiopia, Article 40 of the Federal Democratic Republic of Ethiopia Rural Land Administration and Use Proclamation of 2024 reaffirms the orthodoxy that rural land disputes may be resolved through negotiation, mediation/conciliation, or adjudicated in the regular court having jurisdiction. Administrative bodies shall not

[2] [2011] ZWHHC 7.

[3] [2021] ZWMSVHC 17 (10 March 2021).

[4] Lankono and Forkuor (2023).

be prevented from entertaining administrative issues arising from land matters. Article 7 of the Afar National Regional State Rural Land Administration and Use Proclamation No. 49/2009 provides that:

> Land disputes arising between pastoralists shall be settled under the customary dispute settlement system. A party who is aggrieved with the decision of the elders under sub article 1 of this article may apply to the woreda court. A party who is aggrieved with the decision of the woreda court under sub article 3 of this article may appeal to the high Court. A party who is aggrieved with the decision of the High Court under sub article 4 of this article may appeal to the Regional Supreme Court. The decision of the Regional Supreme Court shall be final. The decision of the Regional Supreme Court may be revised by the Cassation Court where there is fundamental error of law in the decision of the lower court.

In Zambia, traditional institutions play a significant role in dispute resolution and access to justice and are recognised by the Constitution and state legislation. Article 118(2)(d) of the Constitution recognises traditional dispute resolution mechanisms and mandates their promotion. Additionally, the Local Courts Act implicitly authorises traditional institutions to arbitrate or settle disputes with the consent of the parties to the dispute.

Although the work of traditional hierarchies in dispute resolution is widespread, there is scant primary evidence of this important function except for anecdotal evidence from case studies and judicial decisions of disaffected parties to indigenous arbitration. Examples of case studies in this regard include Assaga's work on traditional land dispute resolution mechanisms in Ghana[5] that explores

> the importance of traditional dispute resolution institutions in the management of land-related disputes in southcentral and western Ghana, drawing on data collated from 380 farming households operating 746 plots. The results show that contrary to the conventional thinking that traditional institutions are anachronistic and not fit for purpose, they remain strong and a preferred forum for land dispute resolution (proving resilient and adaptable), given the changing socio-economic and tenurial conditions.[6]

Hebnick's overview of land and grazing disputes in Namibia[7] chronicles the overlapping authority of the Communal Land Boards and Traditional Authorities, both of which are charged by the Communal Land Reform Act with dispute settlement regarding access to, and use of, communal land.

The other means through which the salience of indigenous land tenure disputes can be demonstrated across Commonwealth Africa is the review of their decisions by state courts considered in Section III of this Chapter. That review reveals that indigenous land dispute matters feature prominently. Unfortunately, it is also true that substantial decisions by families and communities are not reviewed and remain the principal means of dispute settlement in Africa. These decisions are not recorded,

[5] Asaaga (2021), pp. 10, 143. See also, Kuusaana et al. (2013), pp. 14–27.

[6] Asaaga (2021), p. 1.

[7] Hebnick (2021).

and even if they were, they are often motivated by a desire for reconciliation and social peace.

There is also no clear evidence of whether these decisions relate to privatisation concerns, especially in states where it leads to tenure changes. For example, there is little evidence in Nigeria of how traditional authorities manage tenure disputes of customary rights of occupancy beyond their role in assigning occupancy rights. However, the embedded nature of these occupancy rights in indigenous communities suggests that indigenous hierarchies play a key role in their management. There are also African states such as Tanzania, Uganda, and Ghana, where, as the next section reveals, indigenous chieftaincy and other hierarchies play a role in dispute settlement in addition to the localised and statutorily enabled dispute settlement bodies. Again, there is little evidence of how that process unfolds.

Ultimately, more work must be done to unearth evidence of the impact of family and communal arbitration of indigenous land disputes in African states.

3 Local Land Management Institutions and Dispute Settlement of Indigenous Land Tenure Disputes

As stated above, the establishment of 'alternative' local land institutions for the management of indigenous land tenure outside the control of traditional authorities and populated by different village stakeholders, including women, is the preferred means of dispute settlement by several African states.

Our first example is the Ugandan Land Act, which established an Area Land Committee and charged this Committee with many functions, including adjudicating upon and deciding questions of customary land ownership. Incidental powers are also granted, which are necessary for exercising the powers to recommend issuing a certificate of customary ownership and to conduct hearings. The committee may also determine whether customary law applies to the specific land which is the subject matter of the application for a certificate of customary ownership. Furthermore, in determining rights under the customary land tenure system in terms of land ownership, they decide whether a certificate should be issued. In the process, the committee has powers to determine whether there are any third-party rights not amounting to ownership, inclusive of a lease, right of occupation, use, charge, pledge, or other encumbrance of a third party, whereupon they would record the nature, the incidents, and extent of the property rights and advise the board upon any relevant question. The committee is further charged with the duty to safeguard the interests and rights in land, which is the subject of an application by women, absent persons, minors, and persons with disabilities.

In exercising its functions, the committee may conduct and refer any question to the institution of a customary nature for advice. It is this last part which formed the specific attack of the petitioners on the question of whether it was sufficient to merely refer a question to any customary institution for advice, which advice may or may not be considered at the discretion of the Area Land Committee. Specifically, the petitioners submitted that the clan and customary institutions are best placed to handle such disputes and issues relating to customary tenure. Another institution is the District Land Board, which is charged with the power to issue customary ownership certificates on the recommendations of the Area Land Committee, which forwards the application after conducting a series of investigations. The Board has the power to accept the recommendations and issue the certificate or refuse to issue it. The Board may give reasons for the grant or refusal. An appeal lies to the Land Tribunal from a decision of the District Land Board in matters of application for registration of customary Land ownership. Section 74 of the Ugandan Land Act establishes a district land tribunal whose jurisdiction includes determining disputes relating to the grant, lease, repossession, transfer, or acquisition of land by individuals, which presumably would include customary land.

Tanzania is the second example. The Village Land Act 1999 and Courts (Land Disputes Settlements) Act 2002 establish 'local' dispute settlement bodies whose jurisdiction, appointment, and personnel qualification, powers, and appeal process are instructive and serve as examples of state-supported local institutions. The CLDS Act and the Village Land Act establish a Village Land Council of seven people, three of whom shall be women, nominated by the Village Council and approved by the Village Assembly. The functions of the Village Council are to mediate between and assist parties to arrive at a mutually acceptable resolution on any matters concerning village land, including land-sharing arrangements with other villages and land-sharing arrangements between pastoralists and agriculturalists. A dissatisfied party can appeal to the Ward Tribunal, a court in terms of the Ward Tribunals Act of 1985, with a membership of between four to eight members, three of whom shall be women. The general jurisdiction of the Ward Tribunal is mediatory, which assists parties in a dispute to arrive at a mutually acceptable solution. Its specific jurisdiction is to 'enquire into and determine disputes arising under the Village Land Act 1999 and the Land Act 1999. The mediatory jurisdiction of the ward tribunal is anchored in customary principles of mediation, natural justice— when customary principles do not apply— and principles and practices of mediation that members of the ward tribunal have been trained in'.[8] The informal nature of the Ward Tribunals is bolstered by the prohibition of lawyers, even though relatives of parties can appear before the Tribunal. Mediation outcomes must be in writing and include remedies such as recovery of possession of land, specific performance of contracts, injunctions damages, compensation costs payments, and any order that the justice of the case requires. The District Land and Housing Tribunal (DLHT) is the next body to which appeals are made from the Ward Tribunal. The DLHT operates as a court of superior record. The High Court (Land Division), the Court of Appeal, and the Tanzanian Supreme Court are in ascending hierarchy.

It is plausible that the informality of the Village Land Council at the lowest rung of the dispute settlement process is appropriate for indigenous land tenure because

[8] See sect 13(3) of the CLSD.

it is similar in many respects to the exercise of chiefly authority, but different, because it is more stakeholder-based and somewhat independent, and potentially capable of protecting women. The importance of the Village Council is underscored by its role in adjudication and boundary setting. It is likely that the Council has resolved several disputes. Providing an original and appeal process to the Ward Tribunal provides a safe space for dissatisfied villagers. In addition, the hybrid character of Ward Tribunals is commendable because they mimic customary dispute settlement and features of state judicial systems. Pedersen argues that Tanzanians have embraced the state-supported local dispute settlement systems that, in addition, appear to work in harmony with the customary dispute settlement of elders who withdraw disputes before the Ward Tribunals and the District Land and Housing Tribunals.[9] There is also rich literature on the limited effectiveness of Tanzania's localised dispute settlement mechanisms.[10]

4 The Unlimited Jurisdiction of State Courts Over Indigenous Land Tenure Disputes

This section reviews the jurisdiction handed to state courts, including customary and indigenous courts, which includes the resolution of land conflicts. These courts are usually different from the tenure bodies considered in the previous section. The unlimited jurisdiction of state courts, as a feature of liberal democratic states, subordinates indigenous legal orders in two significant ways. First, citizens approach state courts that, in the exercise of their unlimited jurisdiction, entertain actions that may be related to the privatisation of indigenous land tenure. Understandably, land tenure conflicts make up a significant portion of these disputes. The extent to which they turn to indigenous law to resolve these disputes is unclear. However, there is evidence from Nigeria, as seen in Chapter 3, that Nigerian courts have adjudicated the nature and extent of deemed customary rights of occupancy as a continuation of customary law. The other means through which state courts subordinate indigenous dispute resolution mechanisms is judicial review of outcomes of indigenous arbitral processes. Nigeria and Ghana are good examples of this process.

Nigerian courts have long accepted 'an arbitration of a dispute founded on the voluntary submission of the parties to the decision of the arbitrators who are either the chiefs or elders of their community, and the agreement to be bound by such decision or freedom to resile where unfavourable'.[11] Several customary arbitration outcomes that were reviewed by Nigerian courts predominantly focus on land tenure

---

[9] See Pedersen (2018), pp. 176, 163–183.

[10] See Ngemera (2016).

[11] *Agu v Ikewibe* (1991) 3 NWLR (Pt 180) 385, 407. See the following literature on customary arbitration in Nigeria: Igbokwe (1997), p. 41: 201; Elombi (1993), pp. 803–824; Allot (1988), pp. 231–234; and Ikeyi and Maduka (2014), pp. 328–349.

issues, including *Okporowo v Okpokam*;[12] *Nwosu v Nwosu*;[13] *Igwego. Ezeugo*;[14] *Eke v Okwaranyia*;[15] *Egesimba v Onuzuruike*; [16] and *Onyenge v Ebere.*[17] In *Ohiaeri v Akabeze,*[18] the customary arbitration was made by the traditional ruler and his cabinet. It was the chiefs and elders of the town in *Agu v Ikewibe,*[19] who presided over the customary arbitration. In *Okere v Nwoke*,[20] the customary arbitration was reached by the Parents/Teachers Association, that consisted of elders. In *Igwego v Ezeugo*,[21] two bodies, a peace committee and another traditional body, the Uku-na-Umuogu, were involved in arbitrations. In *Awosile v Sotunbo*,[22] a traditional ruler and his chiefs conducted the arbitration. In *Ojibah v Ojibah*,[23] it was the Obi of Onitsha-in-Council of Chiefs, while in *Okpuruwu v Okpokam*,[24] it was the Ofutop Council of Chiefs. In *Inyang v Essien*,[25] those who acted as arbitrators were councillors of the District Council. In *Ekwueme v Zakari*,[26] the arbitrators were a group of interested persons, possessing no authority recognised by any native law or custom. In *Obioha v Akukwe,*[27] it appears that the Court would have recognised the decision of a 'Local Arbitration Panel' headed by a traditional ruler. The various indigenous authorities in Nigeria are just an example of the widespread practice of indigenous arbitration over land disputes. In recognising customary arbitration, Nigerian courts have also recognised the paranormal dimensions of the customary arbitration process. Specifically, Nigerian courts have recognised the resort to traditional oaths such as juju swearing and the consultation of oracles and fortune tellers as legitimate forms of customary arbitration. Whatever doubt that existed regarding these forms of customary arbitration has been resolved by the Supreme Court in the recent case of *Onyenge v Ebere.*[28] In order to resolve a dispute over the pledge of a piece of land, the disputing parties took the matter to a juju priest of the 'Akpam Juju' in Obuzo in Asa Local Government Area of Abia State. The party claiming that the land was a pledge was ordered by the juju priest to swear an oath on a juju provided

---

[12] [1988] 4 NWLR (pt. 90) 554.
[13] (1996) 2 NWLR (pt. 428) 64.
[14] (1992) 6 NWLR (pt 249) 561.
[15] (2001) 12 NWLR (pt. 726) 181.
[16] [2002] 15 NWLR (pt. 791) 466.
[17] [2004] All FWLR (Pt 219) 981.
[18] (1992) 2 NWLR (Pt 221) 1.
[19] (1991) 3 NWLR (Pt 180) 385.
[20] (1991) 8 N.W.L.R. (pt. 209) 317.
[21] (1992) 2 N.W.L.R. (pt. 249) 561.
[22] (1992) 5 NWLR (pt. 234) 514.
[23] (1991) 5 NWLR (pt. 191) 296.
[24] [1988] 4 NWLR (Pt.90) 554.
[25] (1957) 2 FSC 39.
[26] (1972) 2 ECSLR 631.
[27] [2000] 5 NWLR (Pt. 658) 611.
[28] [2004] All FWLR (Pt 219) 981.

by the opposing party. The opposing party refused to abide by this decision, but instead summoned the first party to appear before a foreign juju 'Ogwugwu Akpu' of Okija in Anambra State. The juju was brought down from Okija to Asa and placed on the disputed land. The party claiming the land was a pledge, took the oath and survived the customary one year of oath-taking and celebrated the one year of survival in compliance with the custom of Asa-Ukwu people. By their custom, the party that survived the oath-taking became entitled to the possession of the land in dispute. The other party asserted that the survival of the oath was not conclusive because the successful party did not enter the land, and the Okija juju priest had stated that the oath-taking party would not be harmed if they did not enter the land. Anxious to enforce the terms of the arbitration, because the losing party refused to leave the land, an action was commenced at the Ukwa Customary Court confirming they were entitled to the piece of land, and a perpetual injunction. The plaintiffs were awarded a judgment by the Ukwa Customary Court. Ultimately, the matter got to the Supreme Court, and that court affirmed the award of the Ukwa Customary Court. Niki Tobi JSC, who read the lead judgment of the Court, said:

> This court recognizes oath-taking as a valid process under customary law arbitration. In *Ume v Okoronkwo* … , Ogwuegbu JSC held that oath taking was one of the methods of establishing the truth of a matter and was known to customary law and accepted by both parties. I am bound by that decision.[29]

There appears to be no better example of a customary arbitration process that depends entirely on the native law and custom of the community than a process of a community that houses the juju. The nature of the traditional oath is such that the swearer invokes the juju usually before witnesses by affirming the truth of his declaration or assertion and stating that should be wrong, the juju should kill him after the agreed period, which is usually after one year.[30] While this is a general definition, it is important to remember that every juju or oracle has its own rules and regulations,[31] which are read out by the custodian of the juju or oracle in the course of administering the oath. In many cases, the rules and regulations are intricately woven with the community where the juju or oracle is located. It is after the agreed period that the custodian announces the facts as they are, and the consequences take effect. Generally, if the swearer survives the oath, his declaration takes effect. Thus, if he declares that a piece of land or other property is his own, survival of the juju constitutes him as the owner of the juju without more. However, the rules of the juju, as stated above, is critical in determining the consequences of survival or otherwise.

---

[29] Ibid. p 998.

[30] See Oba (2008), p. 139.

[31] In *Uzoewulu v Ezeaka* [2000] 14 NWLR (Pt. 688) 629, the Juju in question was to be sworn to, which automatically confers ownership on the swearer. In other instances, the swearer usually waits for a year for a manifestation of the juju or oracle.

Ghana has formalised its recognition of customary arbitration by the promulgation of the Alternative Dispute Resolution (ADR) Act of 2010.[32] The requirements of a valid customary arbitration include consent to the customary arbitration[33] and that a party that has commenced an arbitration cannot resile from such process.[34] Customary arbitration is obligated to follow the rules of natural justice and fairness.[35] An award in a customary arbitration is binding between the parties and those claiming through them without the need to register the award.[36] Furthermore, an award can be enforced in the same manner as a court judgement.[37] There is also judicial review of customary arbitration on the grounds of breach of natural justice; a miscarriage of justice has occurred; and the award is in contradiction to known customs of the concerned area.[38] Litigants who came before these courts urged in some cases that the matter before the court had been deliberated upon by a traditional institution and urged the court to recognise these decisions, thereby making them decisions of the regular courts, which would invoke the principle of estoppel denying the re-litigation of the same issues between the same parties. Customary law, as a complete normative system, has several dispute resolution systems that in some instances would qualify as regular courts in every sense, especially because they were backed by the force of the community and other methods of enforcement, including banishment, ostracism, and excommunication. Thus, decisions reached by these institutions were enforceable, even if sometimes with the assistance of the supernatural. Other dispute resolution mechanisms arise from the nature of social relations but were not part of the recognised judicial structure of the relevant communities. The decisions of these dispute settlement mechanisms were based entirely on the voluntary conduct of the parties. They would decide to submit their dispute to a third party and to abide by or resile from the decision of the third party. While customary law in its ordinary parlance involves communities organised by reason of biological ancestry, other communities have arisen, such as Nigeria, by reason of geographical contiguity, trade, and business that have developed a normative system complete with accepted dispute resolution mechanisms. In many cases, litigants urge courts to abide by the decisions of these dispute resolution mechanisms, as resolving the dispute in the same way that members of a community would urge a court.

Kenya has also begun a process for formalising customary arbitration pursuant to Article 159(2)(c) of the Constitution, which provides that in exercising judicial authority, the judiciary is to be guided by some principles, including the promotion of alternative forms of dispute resolution, including reconciliation, mediation,

[32] Customary arbitration is provided for in part three of the ADR Act.

[33] See sects 89 and 90 of the ADR Act.

[34] See sect 105 of the ADR Act.

[35] See sect 93(1) of the ADR Act.

[36] See sect 109 of the ADR Act.

[37] See sect 111 of the ADR Act.

[38] See sect 58 of the ADR Act.

arbitration, and traditional dispute resolution mechanisms (Judiciary 2023). Article 159(3) limits the use of TDRMs by requiring that their use shall not: contravene the Bill of Rights; or is not repugnant to justice and morality, or result in outcomes that are repugnant to justice or morality. Furthermore, the use of TDRMs should not be inconsistent with the Constitution or any written law. Several decisions by Kenyan courts, such as *Erastus Mutuma v Mutia Kanuno*,[39] *Republic v Mohamed Abdow Mohamed*,[40] and *Sakayo Mwimbi v Kithombe Katumi*[41] have examined the legality of customary arbitration.

The idea that access to courts is a fundamental human right for citizens of these states is a recognised feature of the right to fair trial. The consequence of unlimited judicial review ensures that parties to an indigenous land tenure dispute can largely opt for a state court and disregard indigenous arbitral institutions. First, as noted above, there is no exclusive jurisdiction over indigenous land tenure granted to indigenous authorities that would result in state courts yielding their jurisdiction to indigenous authorities. Second, a mechanism through which African states try to foster recourse to 'local courts' for the adjudication of indigenous tenurial disputes requires the use of alternative dispute mechanisms, including indigenous arbitral institutions as a condition precedent to the jurisdiction of regular courts. Thus, Section 98(1) of the Ghana Land Act provides that an action concerning any land or interest in land in a registration district shall not be commenced in any court unless the procedures for the resolution of disputes under the Alternative Dispute Resolution Act, 2010 (Act 798) have been exhausted. In *Lobi v Kagwera*,[42] a Malawian High Court delivered a ruling on a claim for an interdict against the trespass of an inherited piece of land situated in Kagwera Village, Traditional Authority Masumbankhunda in Lilongwe Districtbut declined to take up the matter. The contention was whether the chief of the village had allocated the piece of land to the alleged trespasser. It emerged that the dispute had been adjudicated by the Senior Chief of Masumbankhunda, who ruled against the claimant. One of the key issues for determination is whether this case should have been first commenced in a customary land tribunal. The issue arises within the context of the Customary Land Act, 201, which provides, among other matters, a dispute settlement system for the adjudication of disputes about customary land in Malawi. Part VII of the Act makes provision for the settlement of disputes relating to customary land. Section 44 of the Act establishes in every traditional land management area a customary land tribunal to adjudicate on any dispute concerning customary land in the area. In terms of Section 45 of the Act, appeals from a customary land tribunal are directed to a district land tribunal. A person aggrieved by a decision of a district land tribunal may appeal to a central land board. Finally, Section 49(5) of the Act provides that a party dissatisfied with a decision of the Central Land Board has a right to appeal against

[39] [2012] eKLR.

[40] [2013] eKLR.

[41] [2019] eKLR.

[42] [2023] MWHC 60.

the decision of the High Court. The Court upheld the contention of the defendant that as far as the matter did not go through the subordinate courts, it was premature.

5 Conclusion

Credible records of the resolution of privatisation-related tenure disputes in the formal and informal adjudicatory hierarchies in African states would have enabled an articulation of principles of indigenous land tenure in many respects. Issues like the responsibilities that follow members of the community who have become entitled to communal land *qua* their membership in these communities would have been clearer. Although there are judgements of the assessments of outcomes of indigenous arbitration in several states, it remains an ongoing process of identifying the judgements that are related to privatisation. The widespread lack of records of indigenous arbitration of tenure across Africa localises principles of indigenous land tenure, leaving us without insight into the process and substance that indigenous authorities contribute to tenure disputes and their influence on indigenous law.

References

Allot AN (1988) Customary arbitrations in Nigeria: a comment on Agu v Ikewibe. J Afr Law 42:231–234

Asaaga F (2021) Building on 'Traditional' Land dispute resolution mechanisms in rural Ghana: adaptive or anachronistics. Land 10:143. https://doi.org/10.3390/land10020143

Elombi G (1993) Customary arbitration: a Ghanaian trend reversed in Nigeria. Afr J Int Comp Law 5:803–824

Hebnick P (2021) Land and grazing disputes and overlapping authorities in Namibia. J Legal Plural Unoff Law 53

Igbokwe V (1997) The law and practice of customary arbitration: Agu v Ikewibe and applicable issues revisted. J Afr Law 41:201

Ikeyi N, Maduka T (2014) The Binding Effect of a Customary Arbitration Award: Exorcising the Ghost of *Agu v Ikewibe*. J Afr Law 58:328–349

Judiciary K (2023) Alternative Justice Systems Baseline Policy and Policy Framework. Available at https://www.judiciary.go.ke/download/alternative-justice-systems-baseline-policy-and-policy-framework/. Accessed 27 Oct 2025

Kuusaana ED, Kidido JK, Appiah MN, Obeng Mireku KO (2013) Alternative dispute resolution by chiefs and Tendamba: a case study of Kumasi and Wa traditional areas The Ghana. Surveyor 5(1):14–27

Lankono CB, Forkuor D Asaaga FA (2023) Examining the impact of customary land secretariats on decentralised land governance in Ghana: evidence from stakeholders in Northern Ghana Land Use Policy 130:106665

Ngemera S (2016) Land adjudication process for land rights in mainland Tanzania: is it a remedy to village land disputes? Int J Inf Res Rev 3(12):3422–3430

Oba AA (2008) Juju oaths in customary law arbitration and their legal validity in Nigerian Courts. J Afr Law 52:139

Pedersen RH (2018) State-orchestrated access to land dispute settlement in Africa: land conflicts and new-wave land reform in Tanzania. In: Zanker O, Hoehne MV (eds) The state and the Paradox of customary law in Africa. Routledge, pp 176, 163–183

The Privatisation of Land Tenure and the Future of Indigenous Law in Africa

Content

1 The Privatisation of Land Tenure and the Future of Indigenous Law in Africa............ 141

1 The Privatisation of Land Tenure and the Future of Indigenous Law in Africa

The question this book sought to address was whether anything remained of indigenous law in Africa in the wake of the privatisation of indigenous land tenure in African states. The answer to this question is that privatisation so far bodes well for African states and therefore guarantees a future for indigenous law. This broad conclusion is a summary of the different outcomes of indigenous law in the 53 states of Africa. It is clear from the analysis in this book that privatisation has changed and challenges indigenous land tenure in Africa. It is not surprising that indigenous law in Africa, as a socially constructed system of law, has mutated and transformed into different forms; some identifiable, others that are not easily identifiable, and yet others are emerging. Indigenous law has adapted to the strong influence of colonial powers. The models of privatisation of indigenous land tenure examined in chapter "Models of Private Interests in Indigenous Land Tenure in Africa" earlier reveal the survival of indigenous land tenure in its individual and communal components. Where African states nationalised all land tenure, they also recognised directly and indirectly some form or another of indigenous land tenure, facilitating their survival in several states. Similar outcomes are evident in other states where recent constitutional design directly recognises indigenous land tenure as part of constitutional property. What appears critical is the question of how well indigenous land tenure has survived so far and the prospects of its better survival as part of a critical and important reality in the long overdue transformation of Africa. At the heart of a strengthened indigenous law are reimagined indigenous communities that can

E. Nwauche, *The Privatisation of Indigenous Land Tenure and the Future of African Indigenous Law*, https://doi.org/10.1007/978-3-032-14881-0_8

contribute meaningfully to Africa's development if underpinned by strong indigenous land tenure systems. Several imperatives are important in this regard.

First, African states must acknowledge that indigenous land tenure is neither exclusively collective nor can it accommodate individual interests. The orthodoxy that an exclusive collective title is crucial in the survival of indigenous land tenure is overstated. The extent of collectivisation and individualism in communal tenure systems often merge and overlap. No system is entirely collective, because individual interests in different forms are important for the dignity, autonomy, and survival of members of the collective. However, individual titles must depend on some form of commons for their survival and connection to provide support for the moral engagement of indigenous communities to provide for their members. It is also a myth that Africa's communal land tenure has long been exclusively collective. There is abundant evidence that all forms of internal and external forces have yielded individual interests within the so-called African communal land tenure. To attribute privatisation of communal land tenure in Africa exclusively to the neoliberal models advocated by the World Bank and other international financial institutions is to ignore the pressures on indigenous land tenure by different forces well before the end of colonialism. These forces will continue as ordinary Africans negotiate their survival and well-being within their communities and states. Fortunately, there is evidence from recent constitutional design, in states like Kenya, of indigenous land tenure owned and managed by the community with distinct possibilities in individual interests. It is true, of course, that considerable obstacles of patriarchy and tradition stand in the path of ensuring adequate individual access to indigenous land tenure, suggesting that several African states ought to engage in the reform of the ownership, management, and access to indigenous land tenure.

Second, the idea of indigenous constitutional property is crucial to understanding indigenous land tenure as collectively owned with individual interests. The notion of indigenous constitutional property provides a framework to work through how collective ownership of indigenous land tenure can align with individual interests. Paradoxically, the understanding of indigenous constitutional property and its meaning is absent from the jurisprudence of several African states, including states like South Africa and Kenya that recognise the equality of indigenous law and common/civil law. Unfortunately, the recognition of an equal status of all laws in African states has not found its way into how several constitutional principles and processes are defined or refined. As stated above, one glaring omission is with respect to indigenous property. Interpreting and reinterpreting the privatisation of indigenous land tenure within a constitutional framework will be of considerable importance. Although the liberal ethos of Africa's constitutional design is recognised, it is also true and long overdue to factor indigenous law into constitutional interpretation and the legal system in a meaningful way. The social aspects of property, which is at the heart of indigenous property, is not a strange path for modern African legal systems to follow in recognising that property facilitates relationships and imposes rights, duties, privileges, and burdens. Constitutionalised indigenous property should also recognise the autonomy and dignity of community members who are entitled to negotiate personal interests within the family and community. Individual rights in constitutionalised indigenous property are crucial in sustaining the unanimous recognition of women's access to indigenous land tenure. Fortunately, different aspects of constitutional indigenous property are changing in several African states, as this book has demonstrated. It is not surprising and instructive that these principles of indigenous constitutional property have arisen in recent constitutional designs in African states. In the majority, however, are older constitutional designs where the lack of constitutional recognition of indigenous law is possibly the reason why ideas of constitutional indigenous property are largely absent. Fortunately, constitutional interpretation in these states could easily recognise principles of constitutional indigenous property. It should be remembered that African constitutions demand autochthonous development of principles, processes, values, and institutions. What privatisation has provided are concrete examples and suggestions of indigenous constitutional property for further development. In articulating the principles of a constitutionalised indigenous property, African states must ensure that principles of common/civil law do not supplant indigenous land tenure and that indigenous land tenure enjoys equal consideration in the future of the laws that emerge from the plural mix of legal orders.

Third, inadequate documentation of indigenous land tenure must be addressed to ensure that indigenous land tenure remains a strong foundation for the normative frameworks of indigenous communities. It was a matter of concern that several African states did not document their land tenure to adequately prepare for privatisation. Decades after, several post-colonial African states do not have significant records of the nature and extent of indigenous land tenure. The cavalier attitude of several African states leaves an inescapable conclusion that these states are unconcerned that privatisation could radically harm indigenous land tenure. There is progress in several states in the use of informal and low-cost means of documentation processes. What has been achieved is insufficient for the enormous task of ensuring that individual interests in indigenous land tenure will fare better in a documented indigenous land tenure system. Documentation is crucial for potentially providing evidence of indigenous land tenure and providing communities and their citizens the capacity to deal with their property as they deem fit.

Fourth, there must be concerted efforts in understanding and supporting the growth of the norm-making features of dispute settlement fora as a means of articulating and refining different aspects of indigenous land tenure. Much is done at the community level in managing disputes arising from privatisation that requires understanding. It is often claimed that unique aspects of the indigenous justice system are reconciliation, speed, affordability, and flexibility, but how indigenous African communities integrate these principles into the management of land tenure systems is not clear. Therefore, institutional reforms in record keeping are needed that enable the growth of jurisprudence on the informal aspects of dispute settlement in African states. In chapters "The Privatisation of Indigenous Land Tenure Development and the Future of African Indigenous Law" and "An Overview of Indigenous Land Tenure in Africa" of this book, we noted the oral nature of indigenous law and the harm that this has wrought on its development. Considerable support for record keeping at least in these forums will assist the growth of jurisprudence around indigenous land tenure and indigenous law in general. Glimpses of how these forums function are evident in reviews of the decisions of traditional justice mechanisms in the state courts of Ghana and Nigeria that point to the virtues of reconciliation, affordability, speed, and flexibility. These potential contributions of indigenous law to the legal systems of African states are of considerable importance and show promise for the future of indigenous law in Africa.

Fifth, certain fundamental aspects of reimagined indigenous communities are crucial for the future of indigenous law in Africa. Reimagined indigenous communities should be democratic, in the sense that governance resides with members of the communities rather than exclusively with traditional hierarchies. That said, while it is easy to wonder at the feasibility of reimagined indigenous communities in view of the tradition-laden and patriarchal nature of traditional leadership in African states, there are several examples, as examined in chapters "Models of Private Interests in Indigenous Land Tenure in Africa" and "Patriarchy, Gender, and Access to Indigenous Land Tenure in Africa" of this book, of the democratisation of the management of indigenous land tenure through the decoupling of traditional hierarchies from tenure management. Multi-stakeholder management of indigenous governance suggests that further democratisation of indigenous communities is possible of addressing fundamental governance issues that improve indigenous lives and therefore enhance the future of indigenous law. Another example of the democratisation of indigenous communities is the unanimous provisions of equal access by women to indigenous land tenure through privatisation legislation, which is very commendable and represents a fundamental contribution to the future of indigenous law. Equal access to indigenous property challenges the dominance of patriarchy that results in the engagement of all segments of the population of Africa's indigenous communities towards their development. It is a fact that there is a wide gulf between the constitutionalised and statutory access for women to indigenous land tenure and social practice in several African states. Ensuring that women have vantage positions in tenure management forums in African states enables them to protect women's access and further the democratisation of indigenous communities. The democratisation of reimagined indigenous communities is well recognised in the orthodoxy of the free, prior, and informed consent of indigenous peoples to third-party access of their property. Such democratic participation recognises the autonomy, dignity, and participation of members of these communities in collective decision-making. These processes are not strange to indigenous communities and find expression in the democratised tenure management processes in several African states. Privatisation must be commended for highlighting the democratic potential and signposts of indigenous communities even if the practice varies from community to community. Democratisation further strengthens the renewal of the moral worth of indigenous communities in a changing world, facilitating how these communities provide solidarity, identity, support, and resources in African states with severe governance and regulatory deficits.

A strengthened indigenous law can only exist meaningfully as a legal order within plural legal systems if African states truly consider indigenous law as an equal legal order to the civil and common law that is a legacy of colonial rule. Norm recognition rules such as the repugnancy clauses are clearly outdated in the context of the constitutional rule of several African states and the equality of persons and legal orders that are implicit constructs of constitutionalism. The equality of legal orders is not a common feature in African states which have long been accustomed to the inferiority of indigenous law. So much needs to be done to convince African legal systems otherwise. This conviction will be the basis for the realisation of the considerable potential and possibility in the subtle and contextual influence and impact of indigenous law on common/civil law. It is important that indigenous law is not imagined as exclusive and off-limits to other legal orders. Far from it. The history of indigenous law is littered with such interactions that have, in many senses, stultified the growth of indigenous law. What is crucial is that African legal orders should treat indigenous law less as an exception and more a substantive player in legal developments.

The reform of different aspects of a legal order, such as indigenous law, is a constant feature and will not abate. In chapters "The Privatisation of Indigenous Land Tenure Development and the Future of African Indigenous Law" and "An Overview of Indigenous Land Tenure in Africa", it is noted and demonstrated that privatisation or the pressures for such processes are as old as Africa. The half-hearted implementation of statutory and constitutional reform of indigenous land tenure in several African states has highlighted urgent need for reform. Therefore, it is important to recognise that reform is normal and will continue as a social process and imperative, sometimes hidden from gaze. Therein lies the future of indigenous law in Africa. It will continue to develop from within and because of outside pressures.

MIX
Papier aus verantwortungsvollen Quellen
Paper from responsible sources
FSC® C105338

If you have any concerns about our products,
you can contact us on
ProductSafety@springernature.com

In case Publisher is established outside the EU,
the EU authorized representative is:
Springer Nature Customer Service Center GmbH
Europaplatz 3, 69115 Heidelberg, Germany

Printed by Libri Plureos GmbH
in Hamburg, Germany